THE FIVE WOUNDS OF JESUS
AND PERSONAL TRANSFORMATION

THE
FIVE WOUNDS OF JESUS
AND
PERSONAL TRANSFORMATION

Joseph A. Grassi
Santa Clara University

ALBA·HOUSE   NEW·YORK

SOCIETY OF ST. PAUL, 2187 VICTORY BLVD., STATEN ISLAND, NEW YORK 10314

ST PAULS

Library of Congress Cataloging-in-Publication Data

Grassi, Joseph A.
  The five wounds of Jesus and personal transformation / Joseph A. Grassi.
      p. cm.
  ISBN 0-8189-0838-6
  1. Jesus Christ—Crucifixion—Meditations. 2 Five Sacred Wounds—Meditations. I.
Title.

BT450.G69 2000
232.96'3—dc21   99-058534

Produced and designed in the United States of America by the
Fathers and Brothers of the Society of St. Paul,
2187 Victory Boulevard, Staten Island, New York 10314,
as part of their communications apostolate.

ISBN: 0-8189-0838-6

Printing Information:

Current Printing - first digit   1   2   3   4   5   6   7   8   9   10

Year of Current Printing - first year shown

2000   2001   2002   2003   2004   2005   2006   2007   2008   2009

Table of Contents

Introduction vii
Reader's Guide ix

PART I
THE WOUNDS OF JESUS IN THE GOSPELS AND ST. PAUL

1. Mark, the Gospel of the Cross 3
2. The Gospel of Matthew 31
3. The Gospel of Luke 51
4. The Gospel of John 71
5. The Letters of Paul 87

PART II
MEDIATORS OF PERSONAL TRANSFORMATION

6. The Mother Who Was Also Pierced 103
7. The Liturgy and Rituals 107

PART III
EXAMPLES OF SAINTS WHO HAVE BORNE
THE FIVE WOUNDS OF JESUS, THE STIGMATA

8. Francis of Assisi, Fool for Christ and First Stigmatic 115
9. Catherine of Siena 129
10. Padre Pio 139

Acknowledgment

This book might not have seen light
without the help and encouragement of
my wife Carolyn.
With her special skill as a poet and writer,
she carefully edited every page and greatly improved
the ability of the book
to reach and move our readers.

Introduction

For centuries, the cross or Christ's crucifixion has been a transforming image. The central action of crucifixion is the piercing action or wounds that cause one's death. The word *crucifixion* (from the Latin *crucifigere)* means *to pierce through* (with nails) and attach to a wooden cross. Yet believers do not worship a dead Christ. The once lethal ugly wounds inflicted in hate have become living resplendent instruments for healing, energy and forgiveness. They are now the Risen Christ's ID present in a believing community. The inner meaning of a cross or crucifix is a living crucified Christ whose wounds have become fountains of love and compassion.

The first purpose of this book is to enable the reader to deeply experience the meaning of the five wounds of Jesus as presented in the four gospels and in the letters of St. Paul.

The second is to find new ways to appropriate this meaning to themselves in daily life. To help in this direction, this book will guide the reader to make use of transformative meditation. It will also provide examples from the lives of men and women who have been revolutionized by the image of the Crucified One. In the following pages, there is a reader's guide for fruitful use of this book.

The impelling motive to write this book arises from my own experience of the power of the image of Jesus' wounds. I have found in this image the energy and drive I needed to transform my own life. Also I discovered how effectively it moved others as I presented it to them in groups or in classes. The use of guided imagery in contemplation proved to be a most valuable instrument in this process. All this made me desire to share with a wider audience what has happened to me and others, confident it will have the same or even greater results.

Reader's Guide

1. The Biblical Studies on Jesus' Wounds

These studies are designed for careful reflection as the basis for later instilling the image of the crucified Jesus in the mind and the heart. All the actual biblical texts should be read slowly and reflectively since they have a power of their own. The ancient method for reading the bible is to involve yourself so deeply that you feel yourself as part of the story. This means that *you are actually there.* This is not a pious fiction but based on the way the text was written. It was designed as a living drama in which the audience is there as part of the action.

As an example, consider the story of God giving the Ten Commandments to Moses from the top of Mount Sinai. In the book of Deuteronomy Moses tells this story to another generation who were not yet alive when Moses received and gave the commandments. Yet Moses said to that later audience:

Hear, O Israel, the statutes and ordinances that I am addressing to you *today.*... The LORD our God made a covenant with *us* at Horeb.

Not with our ancestors did the Lord make this covenant, but *with us, who are all of us here alive today.* The LORD spoke *with you face to face* at the mountain out of the fire. (5:1-4)

I have italicized the words in the text that emphasize the immediate tie to today's audience rather than a past one. In Jewish tradition, someone who listens to this story should see with their inner eyes the fire on the mountain and feel its warmth on their bodies. They should shake and tremble when they hear the thunderous voice of God pronounce the Ten Commandments. Bible texts are not designed merely to provide facts and information but to in-form people with God's energy. They are not fashioned for speed reading or computer scanning. As you read a passage, breathe in the words and images to experience the energy within them.

The Transformational Meditations

These will be an expansion and adaptation of the biblical method described above. They make use of guided biblical imagery to help the reader enter the text and become participants. They help the whole person do this by applying the imagination, the senses and the will.

Preparation:

How *not* to use them: by reading or browsing through them. This may prove intellectually interesting but real transformation only comes about when the whole person is actively involved.

The bible was written for people of faith by inspired writers. In this atmosphere we need to start with prayer so the Spirit of God may move and guide us.

The next step is to place yourself in a relaxed unhurried atmosphere. This is necessary so that guided images can freely flow and obtain their effect. A good way to do this is to focus on your breathing. Count your breaths with your fingers up to ten or more until you find yourself at ease. During the meditations there will be many references to using the breath — an important symbol and bearer of the Holy Spirit (Breath) of God.

Since you will not be performing an academic exercise but looking for motivation and spiritual energy, repeat these exercises so you can go deeper each time. You will know they have obtained their desired result when you find yourself with more motivation, courage, confidence, love and determination in your daily life.

The examples from the lives of men and women will provide a practical guide to see how they changed their own lives and those of the people around them.

Detailed List of Subjects

PART I - THE WOUNDS OF JESUS IN THE GOSPELS AND ST. PAUL
1. Mark, the Gospel of the Cross
Detailed biblical study followed by an example: *Martin Luther King* and a transformative meditation: *Jesus' Transfiguration and Our Own.*
2. Matthew, Identification with the Crucified Jesus
Detailed biblical study followed by an example: *Teresa of Calcutta* and a transformative meditation: *How to Reserve a Privileged Place at the Last Judgment.*
3. Luke, The Power of Remembering
Detailed biblical study followed by an example: *Edith Stein* and a transformative meditation: *The Jesus Prayer.*
4. John, the Mystery of the Fifth Wound in Jesus' Side
Detailed biblical study followed by an example: *Dorothy Day* and a transformative meditation: *How to Perform A Mystical Heart Transplant Operation.*
5. Paul and Configuration with Christ Crucified
Detailed biblical study. The example is that of St. Paul himself. The transformative meditation: *Obtaining a New Mind, that of Christ.*

PART II - MEDIATORS OF PERSONAL TRANSFORMATION
6. The Mother Who Was Also Pierced
Experiencing the meaning of Jesus' Wounds through the one who understood them best.
7. The Liturgy and Ritual
The Wounds of Jesus and the Paschal Liturgy.
Toward a more fruitful celebration of the Lord's Supper.

PART III - EXAMPLES OF SAINTS WHO HAVE BORNE THE FIVE WOUNDS OF JESUS, THE STIGMATA
8. Francis of Assisi, The First Stigmatic
9. Catherine of Siena
10. Padre Pio

Part I

The Wounds of Jesus
in the Gospels and St. Paul

1 Mark, the Gospel of the Cross

Why take Mark's gospel first instead of the usual order Matthew, Mark, Luke, John? This is because Mark's gospel seems to be the first written Greek gospel, even though there is an older tradition behind Matthew. It is also the shortest of the four. For these reasons it is easier to make comparisons between the special contributions of each author to the meaning of Jesus' crucified wounds.

The Beginning Foreshadows the End

As Mark writes, the image of the crucified Jesus accompanies him throughout the gospel. This is especially true at the beginning and end of Jesus' career. After his baptism by John at the Jordan river, Jesus had a private visionary experience in which a thunderous voice of God announced to him, "You are my beloved Son" (1:11). I say "private" because Jesus' true identity as son of God is a secret in Mark's gospel that is not revealed until the end of his life on the cross. It is true that the demons on one occasion cry out, "You are the Son of God!" (3:11). However, Jesus orders them to be silent, since they only know him as a healer with divine power. They can know nothing of God's secret plan to save through the cross.

Following his baptismal experience, Jesus undergoes a period of trial and decision as to what this calling meant: "The Spirit immediately drove him out into the wilderness. He was in the wilderness forty days, tempted by Satan" (1:12-13). Mark unfolds

Jesus' concern in the following verse: "Now after John was arrested, Jesus came into Galilee, proclaiming the good news of the kingdom, saying, "The kingdom of God is at hand." Arrest by Herod, the Roman appointed puppet king of Galilee, was a usual prelude to execution. The large crowds attracted by the Baptist alarmed the king. They could lead to a Messianic uprising. If the king failed to act, the Romans could accuse him of disloyalty and remove him from office. Uprisings of this kind were a constant danger in a country where Messianic expectations lured many people to believe that God would raise a chosen leader to liberate them from a burdensome and humiliating Roman domination.

Seeing that the Baptist, his first teacher, is arrested, what is Jesus to do? Should he retire to safety and stop preaching the coming kingdom of God or should he continue on a path leading to certain execution either by Herod or the Romans? The Romans were quick to arrest any popular leaders who might instigate an uprising. They dealt with them in the swiftest and cruelest way they knew: execution by public crucifixion as a horrible and shameful example to others. Jesus had heard stories about thousands of men who had been crucified in an uprising in the years before his birth. The call to be a "Son of God" implied faithfulness and obedience to continue to preach the good news of the kingdom. But what about his own future and family if this meant risking a horrible death, perhaps within a short time?

Jesus struggled and prayed over this decision in a desert place for forty days. The outcome is described in 1:14 when Mark tells us that Jesus decided to return to Galilee and preach about the coming kingdom of God. This implies that Jesus not only decided to continue the Baptist's mission but to expand it. Previously, the Baptist had remained in the narrow confines of the Jordan river. People (mostly all men) *came to him*, forming a male enclave of disciples who stayed with their teacher and assisted him. Jesus had been one of that group. However, in contrast, Jesus expanded the mission of the Baptist *and went out to where people were*. He taught in the marketplace and peoples' homes. He welcomed men, women and children of every social class. Far from escaping the risk of arrest and death, Jesus began a missionary career that placed him in the shadow of the cross. He knew this very well and this gave special power to his words. His own life became a witness of the truth that he was preaching.

The Unexpected Triumph of Jesus: The Conversion of a Roman Centurion

The end of Jesus' career parallels the beginning. A Roman centurion supervised a contingent of soldiers in the crucifixion of Jesus and two others. He was an experienced executioner and could hardly be considered a sensitive, gentle man. He had learned to inure himself to suffering in order to perform one of the cruelest punishments ever devised in history. The Romans had learned the use of crucifixion from the Greeks and were quick to make use of it to discourage revolutionaries and rabble rousers. Mark's brief account omits details that were known to everyone in order to focus on the central meaning of the event for the gospel reader. Actually, the centurion represents a vast audience of Romans and other non-Jews who would later become Christians through the mystery of the cross. They would see themselves as the converted centurion because he realized that only divine power could effect the unexpected reversal in the meaning of a crucifixion.

To understand this reversal, we must carefully look at both ends of this reversal as Mark describes them.

The First Part of the Reversal from a Human Standpoint

The word "crucifixion" literally means to affix a human being, hands and feet to a wooden cross usually by means of nails. The word "nails" only appears in John 20:24 in regard to Jesus' hands, but they are supposed throughout. Only Luke alludes to

Jesus' feet (24:39-40). The nail *wounds* with their extreme pain and profusion of blood were a very important contributing cause of death and the essential part of execution. The whole process could take place over a few hours or even days depending on the strength of the victim and the desire of the Romans to have as many people as possible learn a lesson from this horrible example. In Mark's gospel, the soldiers nailed Jesus to the cross at nine in the morning (15:25) and Jesus died six hours later at three in the afternoon. Matthew and Luke emphasize the time from noon to three when the sun was darkened. John has Pilate order Jesus to be taken away to crucifixion at noon.

A prelude to crucifixion, as an added torture to weaken the victim was a merciless scourging. At this time, soldiers could vent their anger at revolutionaries by taking turns in the flogging. Jewish law limited the number of lashes to forty, but the Romans had no limits. However, the executioners were not interested in just inflicting pain but in humiliating their prisoners in every possible way. In Mediterranean societies where matters of honor and shame were of utmost importance, public disgrace was worse than death. The first in such a series of episodes was the mocking of Jesus by the soldiers.

In this account, the title "King of the Jews" is used in mockery. Perhaps the battalion took their cue from Pilate when he said to Jesus (no doubt with a scornful smirk), "Are you the king of the Jews?" (15:2). The soldiers proceeded to treat Jesus as a king, a king of fools. They beat on his head with the king's rod of authority, genuflected before him in mock homage, spat at his face and put a wreath of painful thorns on his head as his crown. Just as the military saluted the emperor with the acclamation, "Hail Caesar," they greet him similarly, "Hail, King of the Jews" (15:16-20).

In order to provide as much publicity as possible, Jesus and the other accused victims were led through the streets in a public procession carrying their crosses to the place for executions outside the city. This may be the reason why the place was called "Golgotha," or "place of skulls." Here there were crossroads leading in various directions for travelers making their way to Jerusalem. Among them was Simon a man from Cyrene, a Roman province of Northern Africa. Eventually, Jesus became so weakened that he could not continue to carry his cross without frequent falls. So the Romans forced Simon to help Jesus carry his heavy burden (15:21).

Before being nailed to the cross, they stripped Jesus of his garments and gambled to see who would keep them for sale — perhaps to the family or friends of the condemned. Christian art, for reasons of modesty has almost always pictured Jesus with a loin cloth, but the Romans had no qualms in such matters. Jewish culture was always very careful in matters of nudity, which was regarded as a disgrace even in the family or among friends. They cited the story of God's punishment of Noah's son who made fun of his father when he became drunk and threw off his clothes (Gn 9:20-27). It was the custom of victorious armies to parade their prisoners naked in order to humiliate them. On one occasion, God commanded the prophet Isaiah to go naked and barefoot for three years to warn the people that they would face defeat and humiliation if they did not change their ways (Is 20:2-3).

The title on the cross, "King of the Jews" was originally meant to proclaim to everyone that Jesus was a crazy fool. In all, this appellation is found five times in the passion account, twice with Pilate, once by soldiers mocking Jesus, once in the inscription attached to the cross and finally in the last words of his enemies. The personal insults to disgrace Jesus come from three groups. First, the pedestrians along the public highway ridiculed him by word and gesture as they shook their heads and laughed saying, "Aha! You who would destroy the temple and build it in three days, save yourself and come down from the cross." Then there were the chief priests as government puppet leaders, and scribes, the religion teachers of the people who gave an authoritative atmosphere to Jesus' conviction by shouting, "Let the Messiah, the King of Israel come down from the cross so that we may see and believe" (15:32). This is the cruelest and most sarcastic taunt, for they pose as sincere men in authority willing to believe if Jesus could show some power instead of being utterly helpless on the cross. Finally, even Jesus' companions, the ones crucified on his right and left hand, might have been expected to show some compassion, but they ridicule him in the same way (15:32). Luke's account, we shall see later, has one of these men repent.

In addition to all the above suffering, the greatest affliction of Jesus was his sense of betrayal and abandonment. Judas, one of his chosen twelve companions, had secretly gone to the chief priests and promised to betray his teacher at a time and place when this could be easily done (14:10-11). Later he led an armed troop out in the night to the garden of Gethsemane to identify Jesus by a kiss of greeting (14:44-45). When Jesus was arrested all twelve of his male disciples fled, leaving him alone. The hardest blow to Jesus came when Peter, his chosen leader, denied him three times. The last denial was even with a public oath that he did not know Jesus at all (14:71).

However, Jesus' most severe trial was a feeling that God himself had deserted him. Mark gives special attention to Jesus' last words by noting their exact time, the fact that Jesus uttered them in a loud voice and by providing the actual words first in Jesus' own language, Aramaic, and then translating them for his audience in Greek: "At three o'clock Jesus cried out with a loud voice, 'Eloi, Eloi, lema sabachthani?' which means 'My God, my God, why have you forsaken me?'" (15:34).

The Second Part, the Divine Reversal
from Ignominy to Triumph

"Now when the centurion, who stood facing him, saw that in this way he breathed his last, he said, 'Truly, this man was God's Son'" (15:39). What caused the extraordinary change in this hardened Roman executioner to no longer consider Jesus as a despised revolutionary but as "God's Son?" The text only tells us that the centurion noticed *how Jesus had died.* If we try to look through the centurion's eyes as he stands facing the cross, we can learn some things from the text. He would have seen and heard Jesus when he "gave a loud cry and breathed his last" (15:37). A loud cry from a person at the last ebb of his strength is most unusual. In the scriptures, a loud cry is often a sign of triumph. Such a triumph at the point of death despite overwhelming obstacles by an utterly weakened and humiliated person could only be due to an inner power of God.

However, the centurion does not represent an isolated person from the past in Mark's gospel. He represents Romans and others who listen to the gospel. The passion narrative is not limited to the final chapters in Mark; the rest of the gospel is really an extended passion narrative in which the audience is learning the meaning of the cross. Only from this perspective can we learn what moved the centurion to his surprising conversion and confession. The following elements are among those that prepare readers for the final moments of Jesus' life so they can transform the image of the horrible wounds of a crucified man into signs of healing and salvation.

1. The tragic death of Jesus was not a terrible unexpected mistake. First of all, it was *voluntary.* Jesus knew where he might be headed right from the time after his baptism when his teacher, John the Baptist was imprisoned. Continuing the Baptist's mission would inevitably lead to his own death. Jesus made a deliberate decision to go ahead after forty days of intense prayer and fasting. Only a few days before his death he confirmed that decision after another period of intense prayer in the garden of Gethsemane. He knew well that the Jerusalem capital was the stronghold of his enemies. He could have turned back at this time. Yet he chose to go ahead although he shuddered in anguish as he imagined the horrible sufferings that awaited him. He begged his Father to take away the terrible trial ahead, but he also prayed for the strength to do what his Father asked of him. He prayed, "Abba, Father, for you all things are possible; remove this cup from me; yet, not what I want, but what you want" (14:36).

2. Secondly and most important, his death was not an accident but what God wanted: "not what I want but what you want." This does not mean that God wanted him to die but that God wanted him to follow his call to be a prophet even if it might lead to death. In this way it was "the plan of God" and not accidental. If God's call and power were behind the events leading to his death, then the horrible tragedy of the cross could be reversed in meaning and turned into God's instrument of salvation.

3. Connected to this theme of God's plan is Mark's description of the events leading to the cross as a fulfillment of the scriptures. The Jewish people considered these writings as not only history but revealing God's plan for the world. They forecasted the future because the way that God acted in the past revealed how he would act in the future. When Jesus was arrested, this was the first step leading to his death. He said to his disciples and his captors, "Let the scriptures be fulfilled" (14:49). What were the scriptures foretelling by indicating that God completely reverses humiliation and defeat by turning them into victory and exaltation? Mark tells us what they were foretelling in this case by referring to Jesus as *Son of Man* fourteen times in his gospel.

This *Son of Man* is found in its Aramaic form in Daniel 7:13. It occurs during a vision of this prophet about the most disastrous and humiliating experience of the Jewish people. The time was from 167-164 BC when the Greek emperor Antiochus Epiphanes closed God's Temple in Jerusalem and desecrated it by burning pig bones on the altar. This was almost a "death of God" experience as the abode of their God and protector was taken from them. The emperor also tried to destroy traditional Judaism by prohibiting the circumcision of children and doing away with Jewish festivals and ritual practices. Many Jews were put to death when they refused to obey the government.

Daniel's vision describes a great judgment scene in heaven where God completely reverses the sufferings of his people. A figure "like a Son of Man" (or human being) representing the people of

Israel comes before God's throne and he grants him / them freedom and victory over their enemies:

> I saw one like a Son of Man coming with the clouds of
> heaven. And he came to the Ancient One and was pre-
> sented before him. To him was given domination and
> glory and kingship, that all peoples, nations and lan-
> guages should serve him. (Daniel 7:13-14)

This victory took place in history when a revolt of the Jews
won a surprising victory over the Greeks and reopened the Temple
once more for worship. The Jewish people to this day celebrate this
victory with the feast of *Hanukkah* in mid-December for eight days.
It proclaims that no power on earth can be victorious over God
and his people.

The Son of Man descriptions in Mark portray the extremes
of humiliation and exaltation as Jesus duplicates the experiences
of his people. For example, Mark writes, "The Son of Man must
undergo great suffering, and be rejected by the elders, the chief
priests, and the scribes and be killed" (8:31). On the opposite extreme, this Son of Man will be with God in glory at the time of
judgment. Jesus says, "Those who are ashamed of me and my
words, of him will the Son of Man also be ashamed when he comes
in the glory of his Father with the holy angels" (8:38). The extremes
will be most evident through the cross where the cruel, ugly wounds
inflicted by his enemies become resplendent sources of healing and
forgiveness.

4. The helpless death of Jesus becomes a powerful voluntary
sacrifice. In the biblical tradition, anyone who obeys and listens to
God's call or invitation becomes an open conduit of God's grace
to the world. When this is done to the point of death it is considered a sacrifice. When offered by someone close to God, it takes
on even greater significance. Jesus is so close to God that he calls
him *Abba,* the Aramaic family term for a human father (14:36).
In Jewish thought every such sacrifice required the sign of blood

flowing to the ground. In the case of Jesus, the audience would perceive the blood flowing from Jesus' gaping wounds as such a sign.

5. The most important sacrifice in Jewish ritual took place once a year, on the day of Atonement, *Yom Kippur*, when the high priest pushed aside the separating veil and entered into the holy of holies in the temple and sprinkled the blood of sacrifice on the place of the Ark of the Covenant. This was to bring God's forgiveness on his people. Mark's readers would see in Jesus' sacrificial death an extraordinary sign bringing forgiveness not only to his own people, but to the whole world as represented by the Roman Centurion. Just after Jesus' death with a loud cry, "The curtain of the temple was torn in two from top to bottom" (15:38). Only after this event does the centurion proclaim Jesus as God's son.

Mark strengthens this sacrificial view of Jesus' death by connecting another central passage of scripture to the Son of Man when James and John requested special places of power in the coming kingdom. Jesus said to them, "The Son of Man came not to be served but to serve and to give his life as a ransom for many" (10:45). These words refer to the image of Israel as a suffering servant of God found in the prophet Isaiah, especially in chapter 53. When their temple was destroyed in 587 BC by the Babylonians, many Jews were taken away in exile to Babylon. There they reflected on the temple and its sacrifices and concluded in that foreign land that the people themselves were God's own temple. They had not lost the temple sacrifices since their own sufferings, if willingly accepted, could be a sacrifice of atonement not only for themselves but for others as well.

In this connection, it is significant that Mark twice notes the words of false witnesses both before the high priest and when Jesus is on the cross, "We heard him say, 'I will destroy this temple that is made with hands, and in three days I will build another, not made with hands'" (14:58, cf. 15:29). The words convey to the gospel audience an ironic truth: Jesus, after his death will become a new temple created by God to bring his presence and forgiveness to the world.

The Transforming Power of the Wounded Christ

1. The first man to carry the cross after Jesus: "They compelled a passerby, who was coming in from the country to carry his cross; it was Simon of Cyrene, the father of Alexander and Rufus" (15:21). Specific names are not frequent in this gospel. Alexander and Rufus are believers known to the gospel audience. The story hints that Simon, although at first compelled, was so moved by Jesus that he began to take the cross willingly and passed his faith on to his two sons.

2. Worship of a crucified king of fools:

> They called together the whole cohort. And they clothed him in a purple cloak; and after twisting some thorns into a crown, they put it on him. And they began saluting him, "Hail King of the Jews!"
> They struck his head with a reed, spat upon him, and knelt down in homage to him. (15:17-19)

We have noted already that this is part of the dishonoring and abasement of Jesus in the story. However, to the believing audience it has a double meaning. In faith they will later be doing as the soldiers did by bending their knees in worship to a wounded and disgraced yet glorified king of folly.

3. Women take the place of male leaders. Mark's gospel has the trappings of a male dominated society. He even gives the names of Jesus' brothers as James and Joses, Judas and Simon, but for the women he briefly notes, "Are not his sisters here with us?" (6:3). Yet the evangelist realizes that the cross has turned things upside down. Judas and Peter, leaders of the twelve, betray Jesus. All of the twelve flee at Jesus arrest (14:50). When Jesus first called his disciples in Galilee, he had said, "Follow me and I will make you fish for people" (1:17). Yet none of the male disciples in Galilee actually followed him to the cross. Mark seems to be remembering those words when he writes,

She feels alone as she feels the desolation her father felt as a result of fleeing the object of their truth.

> There were also some women looking on from a dis-
> tance; among them were Mary Magdalene, and Mary
> the mother of James the younger and of Joses, and
> Salome. These used to follow him and provided for him
> when he was in Galilee. (15:40-41)

The allusion to following him from *Galilee* connects to Jesus'
call to his first disciples in Galilee to follow him to become fishers
of men. Yet it is only the women who actually do follow him to
the cross and become *fisher women!* Their actual names are mentioned three times: at the cross, at Jesus' burial and at the empty
tomb. Without these women's voices, how could anyone have
known about these key events?

4. A prominent Jewish leader risks his own life to bury Jesus.

> Joseph of Arimathea, a respected member of the coun-
> cil, who was also himself waiting expectantly for the
> kingdom of God went boldly to Pilate and asked for the
> body of Jesus. (15:43)

With the spectacular confession of the centurion, it would
be easy to skip over Joseph of Arimathea. He represents those of
his own people whom Jesus deeply impressed by how he died.
Actually, he ranks higher than the centurion, *for he risked his life*
to go boldly to Pilate and ask for Jesus' body as if he were a close
family member or friend. Pilate might have easily sent him to the
cross also as a suspected accomplice. Yet the power of the cross
prompts him to risk everything.

5. The final transformation, death itself turned to life.

> When he (Pilate) learned from the centurion that he was
> dead he granted the body to Joseph. Then Joseph
> bought a linen cloth, and taking down the body,
> wrapped it in the linen cloth, and laid it in a tomb that
> had been hewn out of the rock. He then rolled a stone
> against the door of the tomb. (15:46)

Mark emphasizes the utter reality of Jesus' death. The centurion was a witness and told Pilate. Joseph took down the dead body of Jesus and wrapped it with haste. There was no time for the usual anointing of the body since the Sabbath (beginning at sunset) was drawing near and there was not enough time to buy the necessary materials. Tombs were frequently enlarged caves. They were often considered as conduits to the underworld, the abode of the dead. Large stones were rolled across the entrances to protect the bodies from animals and grave robberies. The closed stone door was also symbolic of the absolute human irreversibility of death. Only divine power could bring the dead to life.

> When the Sabbath was over, Mary Magdalene, and Mary the mother of James, and Salome bought spices so that they might go and anoint him. And very early on the first day of the week, when the sun had risen, they went to the tomb. (16:1-2)

The women once again take considerable risk in identifying themselves as friends of Jesus in order to perform their last actions of loving devotion. The story emphasizes that the events that followed were not planned or expected by them. It is a matter of surprising divine intervention. The three women even wonder who could possibly move aside the great stone (symbolic of all the powers of death) for them. When they arrive, they find it open and see a young man dressed in a white robe, sitting on the right side. They were startled and alarmed, but the young man said to them,

> Do not be alarmed; you are looking for Jesus of Nazareth, who was crucified. He has been raised; he is not here. Look there is the place they laid him. But go tell his disciples and Peter that he is going ahead of you into Galilee; there you will see him, just as he told you. (16:6-7)

The risen Jesus is identified as the "crucified one." His new identifying ID will be his transformed wounds as he goes again before them as their shepherd.

Configuration to the Cross / Wounds of Christ

In addition to the passion narrative, the whole gospel of Mark lies under the shadow of the cross. In what follows we will select some of those passages that are especially relevant. The gospel contains three Son of Man predictions of the suffering and death of Jesus: 8:31, 9:31 and 10:33-34. Each one of these sections is followed by a set of teachings in regard to discipleship, especially in regard to participating in the meaning of Jesus' crucifixion.

The First Prediction, 8:31: "The Son of Man is to be betrayed into human hands, and they will kill him, and three days after being killed, he will rise again." Following this, Peter rebuked him for such an idea. But to teach a public lesson, Jesus turned, looked at his disciples and said, "Get behind me Satan! For you are setting your mind not on divine things but on human things." Thus, to turn aside from the way of the cross is even a temptation of the devil. Jesus further emphasized this by calling the crowd together with his disciples and saying,

> If any want to become my followers, let them deny themselves, and take up their cross and follow me. For those who want to save their life will lose it, and those who lose their life for my sake, will save it.... Truly I say to you, there are some standing here who will not taste death until they see that the kingdom of God has come with power. (8:31-9:1)

To confirm his prediction of a return in power and to give a foretaste of this, Jesus led Peter, James and John up a high mountain. There he became transfigured in light with Moses and Elijah by his side. A bright cloud, signifying the divine presence then came over them and a thunderous voice from heaven announced to the disciples, "This is my Son, the Beloved, listen to him." This parallels the voice from heaven at Jesus' own baptism. Jesus responded to that voice and began his own way to the cross by continuing his mission, even though John the Baptist had been arrested. Now the disciples are also asked to seriously listen to Jesus' difficult challenge to follow him by taking up the cross.

The Second Prediction, 8:31-32: "The Son of Man is to be betrayed into human hands, and they will kill him, and three days after being killed, he will rise again." The teaching in immediate response to this is in the spirit of the cross as the lowest place. The setting is an argument among the disciples as to which of them was the greatest. Jesus sat down, called the twelve and said to them, "Whoever wants to be first must be last of all and servant of all." Then he took a little child placed it among them; and taking it in his arms, he said to them, "Whoever welcomes one such little child in my name welcomes me." The little child, occupying the lowest rung of power in society also fits the theme of the reversal accomplished by the cross.

The Third Prediction: 9:31-32: "We are going to Jerusalem, and the Son of Man will be handed over to the chief priests and the scribes, and they will condemn him to death; then they will hand him over to the Gentiles; they will mock him, and spit upon him, and flog him, and kill him; and after three days he will rise again." This last prediction has the most precise details about the ignominy of the cross. The chief priests and scribes are mentioned again at Jesus' trial (14:53) and at the crucifixion where they stand by mocking him (15:31).

The teaching response to this passage is most striking and direct. Two of the three most prominent members of the twelve, James and John, came to Jesus with a special request. They were excited because they were drawing near Jerusalem where they expected Jesus to inaugurate his kingdom. They asked him, "Grant us to sit, one at your right hand and one at your left, in your glory."

Jesus replied, "You do not know what you are asking. Are you able to drink the cup that I drink, or be baptized with the baptism with which I am to be baptized?" They answered, "We are able." Jesus then said, "The cup that I drink, you will drink; and the baptism with which I am baptized, you will be baptized; but to sit at my right hand or at my left is not mine to grant but it is for those for whom it has been prepared" (10:35-40).

Jesus' answer — that they do not know what they are asking for — hints that they should really be asking to be associated with him through the cross and not by reaching for places of honor. The matter of sitting at Jesus' right or left can have a double meaning. The only two men the gospel specifically described as being at the "right and left" of Jesus will be the two "terrorists" crucified with him (15:27)

"When the (other) ten heard this, they began to be angry with James and John." Jesus had to warn them that the kingdom was not centered on competition for places of power but on competing for the lowest places of love and service:

> You know that among the Gentiles those whom they recognize as their rulers lord it over them, and their great ones are tyrants over them. But it is not so among you; rather whoever wishes to become great among you must be your servant and whoever wishes to be first among you must be slave of all. (10:42-44)

Once again we see the reversal of human values regarding power in terms of the cross. This is confirmed by Jesus' next statement: "For the Son of Man came not to be served but to serve and give his life as a ransom for all."

This third section of teachings modeled on Jesus' cross ends with the healing of a blind man as they walk up the long road from Jericho to enter Jerusalem. When someone tells the blind man that Jesus will be passing by he shouts, "Jesus, Son of David, have mercy on me" (10:47). The crowds made great efforts to silence him but he persisted in calling louder and louder each time. The evangelist wants the gospel audience to identify with this blind man. Human nature is blind to the meaning of the cross, hidden in the plans of God. The readers must humbly ask that their eyes be opened to see and assimilate the meaning of the events in Jerusalem leading to the cross. With the blind person, they ask, "Teacher, let me see." Jesus responds to each, "Go; your faith has made you whole." Like the blind man, all the listeners regain their sight and *follow Jesus along the way* to the cross.

Two Women Teach the Meaning of the Cross

Chapter 13 is a last testament of Jesus in which he describes the coming destruction of the temple and the events which precede his return. He tells the audience not to be deceived by signs such as earthquakes or so called holy wars against the forces of evil. Instead, believers will be asked to duplicate and follow the way of suffering and even death that Jesus has already undergone: "Beware, they will hand you over to councils; and you will be beaten in synagogues; and you will stand before governors and kings because of me, as a witness (*martyrion*, Greek) to them." As a literary "picture frame" for this teaching, there are two beautiful tableaus of women models preceding and ending chapter 13. They carefully parallel one another to make their impact all the stronger. We will place the parallels in italics.

The Widow's Offering of All She Had

The scene takes place as Jesus sat down opposite the temple treasury watching people deposit their offerings. "Many rich people put in *large sums*. A *poor* widow came and put in two small copper coins, which are worth a penny." Jesus called together his disciples and said to them,

> Truly (*Amen*) I tell you, this *poor* widow has put in more
> than all those who are contributing to the treasury. For
> all of them have contributed out of their abundance; but
> she out of her *poverty* has put in *everything she had,* all
> she had to live on. (12:43-44)

Thus the woman stands for those in chapter 13 who are willing to give everything, even life itself, as a witness to what they believe in. Such a total and personal offering contrasts the partial,
often impersonal monetary offerings of the rich.

The Woman from Bethany Pours Out Her Life with the Ointment

> While he was at Bethany in the house of Simon the
> leper, as he sat at the table, a woman came with an ala-
> baster jar of very costly ointment of nard. And she broke
> open the jar and poured the ointment on his head.
>   But some were there who said to one another in an-
> ger, "Why was the ointment wasted in this way? For this
> ointment could have been sold *for more than three hun-
> dred denarii,* and the money give to the *poor.*" And they
> scolded her. (14:3-5)

This story immediately follows the description of the plot of
the chief priests and scribes to put Jesus to death. The woman's
loving devotion to Jesus directly contrasts with his enemies' plot
to kill him. The precious oil of *nard* is only mentioned in scripture in the loving atmosphere of the Song of Songs. Because of its
cost, this ointment signifies the height of extravagance; three hundred denarii would represent a year or more of ordinary wages. The
breaking of the jar and the outpouring of the ointment symbolize
the giving of one's life. Jesus uses the same word, *pour,* in his dis-

course at the Last Supper when he speaks of pouring out his blood (14:24), thus linking the woman's action with that of Jesus' death. Many of those present are angry because they do not understand that this woman is trying to duplicate Jesus' loving personal gift of himself. They consider it a waste of money that could be given to the poor. Jesus says to them:

> Let her alone; why do you trouble her? She has per-formed a good service for me. For you always have the *poor* with you, and you can show kindness to them whenever you wish. But you will not always have me. *She has done what she could.* She has anointed my body beforehand for its burial. *Truly (amen) I tell you,* wher-ever the good news is proclaimed in the whole world, what she has done will be told in remembrance of her.

The parallels between the widow and the woman from Bethany are: 1. The question of the *poor,* with the contrasts be-tween the rich material offerings and the total personal giving. The widow *gave everything she had* and the woman did *what she could.* In this context, both women completely give of themselves as Jesus did. 2. Each story concludes with an emphatic *amen* saying. What the woman from Bethany did was so important that her story will be told wherever the gospel is preached *in the whole world.* This is because the stories illustrate the total giving of Jesus on the cross.

The Last Supper, Conformity with the Wounded / Slain Passover Lamb

"On the first day of the Unleavened Bread, when the Pass-over Lamb is sacrificed, his disciples said to him, 'Where do you want us to go and make the preparations for you to eat the Pass-over?'" This statement and the careful preparations for the Pass-over show that Jesus' actions must be interpreted in view of this feast. The first Jewish Passover was celebrated in Egypt when the lives of all the people were threatened by a deadly plague. Moses told the people to sacrifice a lamb for each family and sprinkle their doorways with its blood. This blood would be a sign that the people belonged to God who would consequently spare them from death (Ex 12:21-23).

The Passover was so important that it was to be celebrated by every generation thereafter: "This day shall be a day of remembrance for you. You shall celebrate it as a festival to the LORD; throughout your generations you shall observe it as a perpetual ordinance." In the biblical tradition to *remember* is to re-experience God's presence and saving action. So Mark describes Jesus' Last Supper in Passover terms because, as the Passover continually recalled the sacrifice of the lamb, the Last Supper would be a way to continually celebrate Jesus' sacrificial death, presence and saving action.

During the meal Jesus took bread, pronounced a blessing, broke the bread and gave it to them saying, "Take; this is my body" (14:22). In the first Passover meal, God instructed the people to (literally) "eat the flesh" of the lamb (Ex 12:8). "Flesh" is equivalent to "body" when rendered in Greek. To eat Jesus' bread, then, signifies union with him as the new Passover lamb of sacrifice. This is confirmed when he takes a cup, gives thanks and shares it with all of them saying, "This is my blood of the covenant, which will be poured out for many." Here Jesus' blood, like that of the Passover Lamb, is a sacrifice that will save his disciples. Eating and drinking, then, signifies an assimilation with Jesus and a willingness to follow him to the cross and even death in loving service of others.

Mark gives special attention to the betrayal of Judas with Jesus' sad announcement beforehand that one of those at table will betray him. The pathos of this event is heightened as one by one each disciple asks, "Surely, it is not I?" The evangelist wants to show that the interior wounds of betrayal would be even more painful to Jesus than his exterior ones. This is a theme that Matthew's gospel takes up in detail. Jesus celebrates his Last Supper and gives his life even for those who will betray him. After the supper, at the Mount of Olives, the extent of this inner wound of betrayal is further revealed when Jesus tells them, "You will all become deserters." Peter protests that this may be true of the rest but not of himself. Jesus then sadly predicts that even Peter, his chosen Rock upon whom he intended to build his future church, will deny him.

Mark, of course, is writing some thirty to forty years after the event. The words are addressed to his contemporary audience to present them with an image of a crucified Jesus, not only with exterior wounds but with deeply felt interior ones from those who betray him. Yet despite this, Jesus continues to give himself in the renewed celebrations of the Passover so that all may have hope, even those who have failed as completely as Peter. About Judas, there will be more in Matthew's gospel.

An Example — Martin Luther King Jr. (1929-1968)

In our brief example, we will highlight some of the events that illustrate Martin Luther King's conformity to the message and life of the crucified Jesus. We recognize the fact that, unlike Jesus who was wholly sinless, Martin Luther King had his flaws and weaknesses. Important for our purposes here, though, is the way he faced a death he knew awaited him if he insisted on pursuing the course he had embarked upon. And there are other similarities too. Immediately we see from the dates above that he died in his thirties, thirty-nine to be precise, for what he believed in, like Jesus, also in his thirties, who went to the cross as a young man. The following are central values or events in his life that are likewise strikingly parallel to those in the life of Jesus:

A Call from God

As a young man in school, Martin was a gifted student, especially in public speech. As a high school senior, he entered a speech contest and won first prize. Because he did so well scholastically, he was able to skip two grades. He entered Morehouse College in Atlanta when he was only fifteen and graduated at age nineteen. He pondered at length about the career he would choose. His excellent academic record qualified him for law or medicine, which were very attractive to him both as opportunities for service and financial enrichment.

Like Jesus he had a "John the Baptist" in the person of his father who was a minister in an Atlanta church. His father had taken important risky stands for justice by helping black teachers receive the same pay as white teachers. He also helped get rid of separate white and black elevators at the city courthouse. Several teachers at Morehouse College who were ministers pointed out to him how a minister could do much to help oppressed people in the areas of hunger, sickness and segregation. His father let him preach a trial sermon at his church when he was only seventeen. The people were so impressed by it that Martin decided to become a minister and started as his father's assistant.

To prepare himself better for the ministry, Martin went to the Crozer School of Religion in Chester, Pennsylvania where he was one of six who were not white out of a student body of a hundred. He graduated in 1951 as top student in his class with a straight A average. A scholarship award of $1200 helped him attend Boston University for doctoral studies. There he met Coretta Scott who was studying to become a concert singer. They were married in Alabama in 1953. His next important choice concerned the place for his ministry. He turned down three college positions and two churches in the north, despite their security, advantages and protection from segregation. Instead he chose a church in Montgomery, Alabama where he could serve people oppressed by Jim Crow laws. He took over his new church in 1954.

Risking Life For Values of the Gospel

Jesus had knowingly chosen a path that could lead to the cross and went ahead even when this became a virtual certainty. When Martin King arrived in Montgomery, it was a "peaceful" town with a population of 50,000. This "peace" was only on the surface, however, since no one dared challenge a system of segregation supported by the law. This situation changed on December 1, 1955 when Rosa Parks was arrested for refusing to give up her seat on a bus to a white person. Martin was part of a group of leaders who decided to start protesting with a one day boycott. This was successful and the group elected King as head of the MIA, the Montgomery Improvement Association. This was the start of his career as a civil rights leader. The group expanded the boycott and people began to walk to their jobs or take taxis whose black drivers offered rides at a minimal rate.

The city officials responded by arresting drivers for almost any reason. King himself was stopped and arrested for "speeding" and thrown into a filthy jail with various types of criminals. From this time on, he began to receive letters and cards threatening him if he did not leave town. Now he knew that he was in real danger. At a weekly meeting he told his people, "If one day you find me sprawled out dead, I do not want you to strike back with a single act of violence. I want you to continue protesting with the same dignity you have shown before." Like Jesus, Martin felt that he could not go ahead on his own strength. He turned to God in prayer and heard an inner voice say to him, "Stand up for what is right, stand up for the truth and God will be at your side forever."

These threats soon turned into destructive acts intended to injure or kill him. A bomb was thrown on his front porch that destroyed the front of his home. His wife Coretta was in the house with their baby daughter, but were saved because they had gone to the back of the house just before the bomb exploded. In September, 1958, he was stabbed in a department store in Harlem, N.Y. as he was signing copies of his book, *Strides Toward Freedom.*

A three-hour operation saved his life. In Birmingham in 1962, the motel where his opponents thought he was staying was bombed. In August, 1963, he addressed over 250,000 Americans from all over the United States who had traveled to Washington to demand equal rights for all Americans of every race, gender, class or creed. In June President Kennedy had asked congress to pass a civil rights bill. It had not yet been passed when he was assassinated on November 22, 1963. King said that his death resulted from a "climate of hate."

Gradually, King became convinced that death was a certainty in the path that he had chosen. His strong stand against the Vietnam war resulted in more attacks on him. In March, 1968, he went to Memphis, Tennessee to help garbage workers on strike for living wages. He returned on April 3rd to deliver an address. He did this despite a warning that he would be killed in Memphis. His plane from Atlanta had been searched for bombs. In his talk, his very last words foreshadowed his coming death:

> It really doesn't matter with me now... Because I have been to the mountaintop. And I've looked over, and I've seen the promised land. I may not get there with you. But I want you to know that we as a people will get to the promised land. So I'm happy tonight. I'm not worried about anything. I'm not fearing any man. Mine eyes have seen the glory of the coming of the Lord!

On the next day, he met with his followers in his second floor motel room and spoke about nonviolence as the only hope to save America. He compared Jesus and Mahatma Gandhi. He told them, "I have conquered the fear of death." Afterwards, he stepped out on the balcony for a breath of fresh air before dinner. A rifle shot from across the street hit him in the face and slammed him to the wall where he fell to the floor. He died in a Memphis hospital about an hour later.

Non-Violence, Jesus and Gandhi

Martin Luther King's last thoughts that morning were about peaceful, nonviolent resistance, a constant concern during his entire ministry. When he received the Nobel peace prize in December, 1964, he said,

> After contemplation, I conclude that this reward which I receive on behalf of that movement is profound recognition that nonviolence is the answer to the crucial political and moral question of our time — the need for man to overcome oppression and violence without resorting to violence and oppression.

King often quoted the gospel and the words of Jesus in regard to nonviolence. At the same time, he greatly admired the practice of *Ahimsa*, the Hindu doctrine of nonviolence expressing belief in the sacredness of all living creatures as espoused by Mahatma Gandhi. He used to call him, "the little brown saint from India." A picture of Gandhi hung on his office wall. This interest in Gandhi's teaching on nonviolent action began when King was in the seminary at Crozer. There he had heard a talk describing how Gandhi had liberated India from the British without using any violence but through peaceful means such as marches, strikes, fasts and boycotts. King came to the conclusion that Gandhi's "war without violence" was Jesus' "way of the cross."

On Martin Luther King Jr's tomb are inscribed the words from his "I have a dream" speech in Washington in 1963: "Free at last, free at last, Thank God Almighty I'm free at last." This freedom was not an escape from this life but freedom from the addiction to power and violence that causes so many people to live in poverty, hunger, oppression and disrespect. This is the same message as that of the crucified risen Jesus.

Transformative Meditation
(See instructions in the Introduction)

Background: Jesus has just predicted that he, the Son of Man, will suffer and die. Peter could not accept this. Jesus rebuked him and addressed the crowds (audience), "If any wish to become my followers, let them deny themselves and take up their cross and follow me. For those who want to save their life will lose it." To give them the strength to accept this difficult saying, Jesus leads them to a mountaintop to be transfigured before them.

Reading: Mark 9:2-8 (Read this slowly, aloud if possible, before beginning)
Six days later, Jesus took with him Peter and James and John and led them up a high mountain apart, by themselves. And he was transfigured before them, and his clothes became dazzling white, such as no one on earth could bleach them. And there appeared to them Elijah with Moses, who were talking with Jesus. Then Peter said to Jesus, "Rabbi, it is good for us to be here; let us make three dwellings, one for you, one for Moses, and one for Elijah." He did not know what to say, for they were terrified. Then a cloud overshadowed them, and from the cloud there came a voice, "This is my Beloved Son; listen to him!" Suddenly, when they looked around, they saw no one with them any more, only Jesus.

Setting: Imagine that you also are fearful after hearing Jesus' statement about taking up your cross and putting yourself at risk for what you believe in. As a disciple you walk up the steep mountainside with Jesus, Peter, James and John. When you reach the top, you look toward Jesus who is praying. As he prays, you see his face change in appearance and become luminous as the divinity within him shines through. You realize that you too will be transformed if you follow Jesus. With Peter you also say, "Lord it is good for us to be here." As you look around you now, notice that the divine light from Jesus' face spreads to the faces of his disciples. They look at your face in wonder for it is also shines with light. For a moment, look at these beautiful rays of light. Feel the warmth and energy as you breathe them in and out.

Then a bright cloud overshadows all of you and suddenly God's thunderous voice proclaims, "This is my Beloved Son; listen to him." You hear the divine voice inviting you to really listen to Jesus' challenge to take risks to follow the call of love. However, now you are no longer fearful. You have experienced the divine presence within and opened your heart wide to that voice's challenge. At this point, stop and ask yourself, "What is it that God wants of me? What risk must I be ready to take in order to follow Jesus more closely?" To answer this make a rapid survey of your family and personal relationships, your career or business, the uses you make of your time. Decide on at least one change for the better that you can make to be more loving at home, among your friends and in the world. Decide on the first step you must make in the near future to put this into action. When the cloud passes, you see only Jesus and your companions as they were earlier. Trust in the light that is still within you and walk down the mountain with confidence and new courage.

2   The Gospel of Matthew

In considering Matthew, we will not repeat what Mark has told us about the image of the crucified Jesus. We will, however, point out those areas where Matthew has a sharper focus. First is regarding the *inner* wounds Jesus suffered by the betrayal of his closest friends, above all, Peter. Matthew's gospel highlights Peter's prominent role among the twelve. For example, only in Matthew do we read the story of Peter walking on water in response to the invitation of Jesus (14:28-33). Jesus also tells him he will be the rock on which he will build his church. He gives him the power of the keys of the kingdom of heaven in the teaching authority "to bind and to loose" (16:17-19).

The Inner Wounds of Jesus

Matthew Highlights Peter's Betrayal and Repentance

More than Mark, Matthew foreshadows Jesus' betrayals in various ways. Jesus strongly rebukes Peter for failing to understand what he was trying to teach him about his coming suffering and death. In a phrase not found in Mark, Jesus tells him, "You are a stumbling block to me" (16:23). In the description of Peter's walking on water, instead of fixing his attention on Jesus, "When he noticed the strong wind, he became frightened, and beginning to sink, he cried out, 'Lord, save me.' Jesus immediately reached out

31

his hand and caught him saying to him, 'You of little faith, why did you doubt?'" (14:20-31)

Peter's Triple Denial of Jesus

Matthew presents Peter's denial and repentance in a much more emotional and emphatic manner than Mark. The best way to illustrate this is by citing Matthew's version. The comparisons to Mark are italicized.

Now Peter was sitting outside in the courtyard. A servant girl came to him and said, "You also were with Jesus the Galilean."

But he denied it *before all of them*, saying, "I do not know what you are talking about." When he went out to the porch, another servant girl saw him, and she said to the bystanders, "This man was with *Jesus of Nazareth.*" Again he denied it *with an oath, "I do not know the man."*

After a while the bystanders came up and said to Peter, "Certainly you are also one of them, for your accent betrays you." Then he began to curse and he swore an oath, "*I do not know the man.*" At that moment the cock crowed. Then Peter remembered what Jesus had said, "Before the cock crows, you will deny me three times." And he went out and cried *bitterly.* (26:69-75)

We notice above that Matthew broadens the audience in the first denial to show how public Peter's statement was. He underlines the very personal nature of the second denial by writing "with Jesus of Nazareth," instead of Mark's version of "one of them." The second denial is portrayed even more strongly by adding, "with an oath." The double statement, "I do not know the man" seems disdainful — that he has absolutely nothing to do with Jesus. However, at the end Matthew heightens Peter's repentance by bringing out its deep emotional tone: "he went out and wept *bitterly.*"

THE TRAGIC BETRAYAL AND DEATH OF JUDAS: HINTS OF REDEMPTION

Judas' betrayal overshadows all the gospel passion accounts. However, Matthew has more about its significance and emotional impact than any other gospel. This is especially true in the story of Judas' death and the personal interaction between Jesus and Judas.

The Last Supper

Like Mark, Matthew has Jesus sorrowfully announce during the meal that one of the gathered apostles will betray him. One by one they distressfully ask, "Surely not I?" Only Matthew has the following ending: "Judas who betrayed him, said, 'Surely not I, Rabbi?' He (Jesus) replied, 'You have said it'" (26:25). As the meal continues after the breaking of bread, Jesus takes a cup, invites them to share it and says, "This is my blood which is poured out for many for the *forgiveness of sins*" (this phrase only in Matthew). Matthew wants the gospel reader to perceive that forgiveness of sins comes from the shedding of blood from the wounds of Jesus on the cross. This option would be open to Judas when he later experiences remorse for his betrayal of Jesus. (See the coming section on Judas' death.)

The Garden of Gethsemane

Mark's version emphasizes Jesus' fear and distress about the horrible pain and suffering he is about to endure. Despite this, he asks his Father for the strength to accomplish his mission. Matthew focuses more on Jesus' interior sorrow and loneliness as he thinks of the betrayals of Judas and Peter and the desertion of his apostles. At the end of the supper Jesus warns them, "You will all become deserters because of me this night; for it is written, 'I will strike the shepherd and the sheep of the flock will be scattered'" (26:31).

Jesus' acute sense of aloneness appears when he says to Peter, James and John, "I am deeply grieved, even to death; remain here and stay awake with me" (26:38). The last words *with me* are found only in Matthew and are repeated again when Jesus comes back to his apostles, finds them asleep and says to Peter, "Could you not stay awake *with me* one hour." Finally, when Jesus returns a third time he says to them, "Are you still sleeping and taking your rest? See, the hour is at hand, and the Son of Man is betrayed into the hands of sinners. Get up, let us be going. See my betrayer is at hand." Jesus willingly goes out to meet Judas who is leading a crowd with swords and clubs.

> Now the betrayer had given them a sign, saying, "The one I kiss is the man; arrest him." At once he came up to Jesus and said, "Greetings, Rabbi!" and kissed him. *Jesus said to him, "Friend, do what you are here to do."* Then they came and laid hands on Jesus and arrested him. (26:48-50)

As at the Last Supper, the italics indicate Matthew's note that Jesus made special efforts to talk with Judas, showing him every possible consideration with the hope of winning him over.

The Suicide of Judas

Since only Matthew records this, we will cite the complete text to underline its full significance.

> When Judas, his betrayer saw that he was condemned, he repented and brought back the thirty pieces of silver to the chief priests and elders. He said, "I have sinned by betraying innocent *blood.*" But they said, "What is that to us. See to it yourself." Throwing down the pieces of silver in the temple, he departed. And he went and

hanged himself. But the chief priests, taking the pieces of silver, said, "It is not lawful to put them into the treasury, since they are *blood* money."

After conferring together, they used them to buy the potter's field as a place to bury foreigners. For this reason, the field has been called the Field of *Blood* to this day. (27:3-10)

To understand Judas, we must first remove the obstacle that his suicide was a serious offense and thus implies his final damnation. However, in the bible a suicide may indicate a noble action to preserve one's own honor or that of one's family or country. Saul, the first king of Israel killed himself after losing a battle with the Philistines. He was afraid they would dishonor him and his country (1 S 31:3-40). Ahithophel was the friend and counselor of king David. They ate together daily. Ahithophel conspired with Absalom, the king's son to overthrow him. When he realized he would not succeed, he went home, put his affairs in order and hanged himself. He was then buried in the family tomb (2 S 17:23). While his betrayal of the king was wrong, the context seems to indicate that his suicide was the honorable thing to do. Consequently he was buried in honor in the family tomb.

Matthew seems to be making a parallel between Judas and Ahithophel. Both were betrayers, one of David, the other of Jesus the Son of David. Both took their own lives by hanging. Judas' death was tragic but not necessarily unredeemed. He probably believed his offense was so horrendous that it was beyond forgiveness. The temple priests told him they could do nothing about it, saying it was his own affair. None of their sacrifices could bring him forgiveness. The triple mention of *blood* in the above story may be an important key. Central to the Last Supper is Jesus' invitation to share his cup, the blood from his wounds on the cross, as a sacrifice for the forgiveness of sins (26:28). There are no limits on the value of this sacrifice nor on its forgiving power. Peter's offense was a serious one, as was that of Judas. However, Peter remembers Jesus' words predicting his failure and trusts in his forgiveness. Jesus also foretold the failure of Judas but Judas could not believe that it he would be forgiven.

Yet Matthew hints that Jesus had a redeeming effect on Judas. The extraordinary personal attention Jesus gave to Judas at the Last Supper and in the Garden of Gethsemane must have affected Judas in some way. He did, after all, openly proclaim to the authorities that Jesus was innocent. Interestingly enough, the chief priests used Judas' money as an offering to buy a special plot of land for the burial of strangers and named it, "the Field of Blood." In a way, Judas' death is a shadow of that of Jesus. According to the closing words of the gospel, Jesus' death would bring the good news to strangers, the *Gentile* world (28:19). Judas' death purchases a field for those "outsiders" who may die in Jerusalem.

THE REVERSE SIDE OF THE CROSS: THE RESPLENDENT WOUNDS OF JESUS

We have just seen that Matthew intensifies Marks' picture of the crucified Christ by highlighting his inner wounds of betrayal and abandonment. At the same time Matthew goes further in proclaiming the reverse side of the cross. He presents a resplendent Risen Christ nullifying the powers of death and effecting the resurrection of believers. Matthew describes the effects of Jesus' death as follows:

> Then Jesus cried again with a loud voice and breathed his last. At that moment the curtain of the temple was torn in two from top to bottom. The earth shook, and the rocks were split. The tombs also were opened, and many bodies of the saints who had fallen asleep were raised. After his resurrection they came out of the tombs and appeared to many. (27:51-53)

The earth shook. Only Matthew describes an earthquake here and in 28:1 upon the removal of the stone at the sepulcher. In biblical imagery, whenever God speaks, the earth shakes. In this case, Matthew is anticipating the other side of the cross: God's tremendous power in disabling the power of death through the resurrection of Jesus. The evangelist is describing the meaning of the cross in terms of the Hebrew scriptures, especially through the famous passage about the "dry bones" in the prophet Ezekiel (37:1-14).

In this passage, God brings the prophet to a vast field filled with dry bones. These represent the "death" of Israel during their exile in Babylon. God tells Ezekiel to prophesy that he will bring life to these dead bones and bring his people back to their own land. As Ezekiel prophesies, he hears a sound like an earthquake as the bones come together again to form human bodies. Then he prophesies further that the breath of life (spirit) will come into the bodies so they will live again. As he prophesies, the breath of life comes into them and they rise to their feet as a vast multitude.

This prophecy of Ezekiel was read in ancient times during the Passover festival. It was often interpreted as describing the resurrection of the dead in the last days. This interpretation is found in a remarkable painting in the Dura Europos synagogue. It portrays a large mountain that is split in two by an earthquake. As a result, many tombs are opened and their scattered bones are brought together. An angel of God breathes new life into these bones and men, women, and children march into Jerusalem. This is the scriptural scene that Matthew has taken. He is telling his audience that Jesus' death and resurrection brings with it the resurrection of all believers.

> Now when the centurion and those with him, who were keeping watch over Jesus, saw the earthquake and what took place, they were terrified and said, "Truly this man was God's Son!" (27:54)

This is a striking contrast to Mark 15:39, where the centurion was moved by the way Jesus died. In Matthew, he is terrified by the earthquake and all the manifestations of divine power in the resurrection of the dead accomplished by the disgrace and pow-

erlessness of the cross. In Matthew it is not only the centurion but
those with him. Matthew wants to include the gospel audience and
all those who experience the power of the risen Christ. Together
with the centurion they *keep watch* over Jesus by fastening in their
minds the image of a resplendent and crucified Jesus.

> After the Sabbath, as the first day of the week was dawn-
> ing, Mary Magdalene and the other Mary went to see
> the tomb. And suddenly there was a great earthquake;
> for an angel of the Lord, descending from heaven, came
> and rolled back the stone and sat upon it. His appear-
> ance was like lightning, and his clothes white as snow.
> For fear of him the guards shook and became like dead
> men. (28:1-4)

Matthew's story of the empty tomb describes a divine epiphany ushered in by a great earthquake. The rolling back of the stone
from the entrance to the tomb is not merely a physical description
of what took place, but signifies the breaking of the impenetrable
seal of death. The angel's appearance in lightning and white garments is a dazzling divine epiphany. In contrast, the guards belong
to the realm of darkness and the dead, more so even than those in
the tomb.

> The angel said to the women, "Do not be afraid; I know
> you are looking for Jesus who was crucified. He is not
> here; he has been raised, as he said. Come see the place
> where he lay" (28:5).

The angel describes Jesus literally as "the crucified one." In
the whole atmosphere of a luminous divine epiphany he is no longer
a lifeless corpse with ugly bleeding wounds. Instead, this is a resplendent crucified Jesus whose wounds are now beautiful signs of
God's transforming power — *he has been raised.* The angel then
instructs the women to bring the message to the other disciples that

he has been raised and will go ahead of them into Galilee where they will see him.

> So they left the tomb quickly with fear and great joy, and ran to tell his disciples. Suddenly Jesus met them and said, "Greetings!" And they came to him, took hold of his feet, and worshiped him. (28:9)

Significantly enough, there is no other expression of worship in this gospel equivalent to the phrase *they came to him, took hold of his feet and worshiped him.* However, on one previous occasion when the disciples had crossed the sea ahead of Jesus, he went up to a mountain to pray and came down in the night walking on the water. The disciples were terrified and thought him to be a ghost. Jesus had to assure them that it was really himself. Then Peter said, "If it is you, command me to come to you on the water." After walking on the water at Jesus' invitation, Peter became afraid as he noticed the waves and strong wind. He then called upon Jesus who reached out his hand and lifted him into the boat. When Peter entered the boat, the wind ceased. Then "those in the boat worshiped Jesus, saying, "'Truly you are the Son of God'" (14:33).

The disciples worshiped Jesus because his miraculous walking on water was a visionary divine epiphany at night and the calming of the storm was likewise a divine manifestation. However, the women had no such sign to prompt them to do what they did. There must have been something about Jesus' person that moved them. Judging from the empty tomb experience, we note they were seeking Jesus the crucified one. Therefore this must be how they saw him. The transformed resplendent wounds were signs of his divinity shining through them.

The only other mention of worship is at the final mountain scene of the gospel in Galilee, where the gospel notes, "When they saw him, they worshiped him but some doubted" (28:17). Here once more it is a vision of the risen though crucified Jesus. The women had already instructed the disciples concerning the message of the angel at the tomb that Jesus, the crucified one, was now risen in God's glory. The disciples also must have seen him in the same way — with his whole body, especially his wounds, transformed in divine light.

The Crucified One Identified with the Poor, Hungry and Oppressed

This identification theme is a special characteristic of Matthew. For example, after the healing of Peter's mother-in-law,

> That evening they brought to him many who were possessed with demons; and he cast out the spirits with a word, and cured all who were sick. This was to fulfill what had been spoken through the prophet Isaiah: "He took our infirmities and bore our diseases" (8:16-17).

In citing this prophecy, Matthew likens Jesus to the figure of the suffering Servant of the Lord in Isaiah, especially chapter 53. This Servant is the faithful Israelite, who like a temple sacrifice, takes upon himself the burdens of his people and offers himself to God for them. The image of Jesus in this guise appears especially in Matthew's Last Judgment scene:

> When the Son of Man comes in his glory, and all the angels with him, then he will sit on the throne of his glory. All the nations will be gathered before him, and he will separate people one from another as a shepherd separates the sheep from the goats, and he will put the sheep at his right hand and the goats at the left. Then the king will say to those at his right hand, "Come you that are blessed by my Father, inherit the kingdom prepared for you from the foundation of the world; for I was hungry and you gave me food, I was thirsty and you gave me something to drink, I was a stranger and you

welcomed me, I was naked and you gave me clothing, I was sick and you took care of me, I was in prison and you visited me" (25:31-36).

After the last verse, in surprise, those on the right ask when they saw him hungry, thirsty, a stranger, naked, sick or in prison. The king answers, "Truly I tell you, just as you did it to one of the least of these my brothers, you did it to me" (40). The name, *the Son of Man,* at the beginning, heightens the identification theme. The Son of Man, as we saw in Mark, is not a solitary figure but includes all of Israel oppressed and humiliated under Greek rule to such an extent that their temple was closed and many people put to death for their beliefs. As such, *Son of Man* was a fitting title for Jesus in the gospel. Those found with this Son of Man when *he will sit on the throne of his glory* (31) will be those who have truly been with him as he identifies with the experience of the poor and oppressed.

The gospel recalls how Jesus, this Son of Man, was often a *stranger* and homeless: "Foxes have holes, and birds of the air have nests; but the Son of Man has nowhere to lay his head" (8:20). He was *hungry* as his disciples resorted to plucking seeds of wheat in the fields, even on the Sabbath (12:1). He was a *prisoner* both of the ruling authorities and of Pilate. He was *naked* when stripped of his clothes before crucifixion (27:35). The whole passion story describes the utter humiliation and suffering of the Son of Man. The three Son of Man predictions in Matthew are always followed by teachings on discipleship to show that believers must be willing to share his lot (16:21-27; 17:22; 20:18-19).

As in the above texts, Matthew's image of the crucified Christ is not only of an individual person. His arms stretched out on the cross embrace all who suffer. The "judgment" scene teaches us that personal service to the poor, hungry and oppressed is a way of loving Christ himself. Veneration of the crucified Christ is inseparable from serving those who make up the community figure of the Son of Man.

There is no mention of particular religious practices or charisms that carry any guarantees in this judgment scene. This is in accord with the Sermon on the Mount, where Jesus said,

> Not everyone who says to me, "Lord, Lord," will enter the kingdom of heaven, but only the one who does the will of my Father in heaven. On that day, many will say to me, "Lord, Lord, did we not prophesy in your name, and do many deeds of power in your name?" Then I will declare to them, "I never knew you; go away from me, you evildoers." (7:21-23)

We note that "Lord, Lord" (*Kyrie, Kyrie*) is a ancient Christian address of prayer. Prophecy in Jesus' name and healing miracles are special Christian gifts. Yet none of these carry any guarantees. Jesus uses the same expression, "Go away from me," that he will use toward those on his left hand in the judgment scene even though they address him as "Lord" and claim they have never turned him away (25:41,44). Jesus' final statement is, "Truly I tell you, just as you did not do it to one of the least of these, you did not do it to me" (25:45).

Jesus' identification with the unwanted and neglected sums up many episodes in the gospel. For example, Jesus begins his career mingling with sinners and being baptized with them in the Jordan River (Mt 3:6); he cures a leper ostracized from society and restores him to the community (8:1-4); he heals two demoniacs forced to live in the community graveyard (8:28-34); he calls a hated tax-collector working for Roman oppressors (9:9); he brings new life and the prospect of marriage and children to a woman afflicted with a continual hemorrhage and avoided by everyone as always unclean (9:20-22); he is amazed at the faith of the foreign Canaanite woman and cures her daughter even from a distance (15:21-28); the blind and the lame, excluded from the temple, dare to come to him for healing in that area (21:14).

A MODERN EXAMPLE: MOTHER TERESA (1910-1997)

I have chosen Mother Teresa because no twentieth century woman I know conforms closer to Matthew's portrayal of identification with Christ. This is the image of a crucified Jesus whose outstretched hands embrace all hungry, poor, unwanted, suffering and oppressed people. To serve and love them is to encounter the living Christ. For a bare outline of her simple life which confounds biographers, I will first quote the obituary published on the Internet by catholic.net.com:

> Mother Teresa, winner of the Nobel Peace Prize, died earlier this afternoon in her convent in India. She was 87. Born Agnes Gonxha Bojaxhiu in 1910 in Skopje, Yugoslavia, she joined the Sisters of Loreto in 1928. She took the name of "Teresa" after St. Thérèse of Lisieux, Patroness of Missionaries (see below).
>
> In 1948, she came across a half-dead woman lying in front of a Calcutta hospital. She stayed with the woman until she died. From that point on, she dedicated the majority of her life to helping the poorest of the poor in India, thus gaining her the name, "Saint of the Gutters." She founded an order called the Missionaries of Charity in Calcutta, India dedicated to serving the poor. Almost 50 years later the Missionaries of Charity have grown from 12 sisters in India to over 3,000 in 517 missions throughout 100 countries worldwide.
>
> In 1952, she founded the Nirmal Hriday Home for the Dying in a former temple in Calcutta. It was there that they would care for the dying Indians that were found on the streets. Mother would see Jesus in everyone she met. It didn't matter whether they were dying of AIDS or leprosy; she wanted them to be able to die in peace and with dignity. For over 50 years she worked selflessly helping the poor. That devotion towards the

poor won her respect throughout the world and the Nobel Peace Prize in 1979.

Over the past two decades, Mother had suffered from heart problems. She suffered a heart attack during a 1983 visit with Pope John Paul II. She suffered another, and more serious heart attack in 1989. It was then that a pacemaker was installed. Just last year she suffered from malaria and was treated for a chest infection. Mother Teresa was a living saint and she will be greatly missed.

THE SPIRIT OF MOTHER TERESA AND HER CONGREGATION

The Fourth Vow

Most religious communities profess three vows: poverty, chastity and obedience. Mother Teresa's Missionaries add a fourth: "Wholehearted free service to the poorest of the poor." No charge is ever asked for or received for any kind of ministration or medicine. The following are characteristics of this service as described by Mother Teresa:

> In serving the needs of the poor the Co-Workers (those lay people associated with the congregation) should give special attention to those who are unwanted and deprived of love. For the worst disease in the world is not leprosy or tuberculosis but the feeling of being unwanted, unloved, and abandoned by everyone. The greatest sin is the lack of charity, the terrible indifference to those on the fringe of the social system, who are exposed to exploitation, corruption, want and disease.

Mother Teresa supported any kind of help for the needs of the poor, no matter how it was given. However, she and her fellow sisters (and brothers in a later community she founded) dedicated themselves to personal, "hands on" service:

> I want people to get involved in the actual work we do, for their own sakes and for ours. I never ask for money, nothing like that. I only ask them to bring their hands to help. Then, when they meet those in need, their first reaction is to do something for them.... I never take care of crowds, only of a person. If I stopped to look at the crowds, I would never begin.

Also, she once said,

> I do not agree with the big way of doing things. To us what matters is an individual. To get to love the person we must come in close contact with him. If we wait till we get the numbers, then we will be lost in the numbers. And we will never be able to show that love and respect for the person. I believe in person to person.

This fourth vow is taken very seriously. Mother Teresa told aspirants to her congregation that they cannot work for the rich. It must be a free service and only to the poor. In the spirit of poverty, the Missionaries have no fixed income. They rely on gifts freely sent in by people. When these gifts are not sufficient to support them and the poor they serve, they go out to beg. Most of the members of her congregation come from a middle-class, well educated background. These young women have known and experienced a far more comfortable life than most in India. Yet they embrace a voluntary simplicity of life, like the poor they serve. This simplicity is true of their clothing, their convents, and their personal possessions.

Mother Teresa herself confessed how difficult it was for her to embrace such a life. At age 18, she had joined the Loreto Sisters and volunteered for work in the Calcutta archdiocese. For twenty years she taught geography in St. Mary's High School. Eventually she became principal there. She enjoyed this life and was dedicated to it. She appreciated the modest comforts of the convent and the privacy of their beautiful peaceful garden. It was such a contrast to the noisy environment and the misery and poverty of so many destitute people who lived on the streets. She had frequently passed by them when she had to leave the convent for business or shopping.

In 1946 at age 38, she was traveling by train to Darjeeling to make her annual retreat when she felt the call to leave this secure life and go into the slums to serve the poorest of the poor whom she had often passed by on the streets. She needed permission to be released from her community, which could only be given by the Pope. It took two years before Pius XII granted her permission to leave her order and serve God as a nun without a convent but under obedience to the archbishop of Calcutta. After this, her first step was to take some limited training in medical work. Soon she began by teaching little children in the slums. Gradually her work expanded to those who were desperately ill on the streets. Other women came to join her and formed the nucleus of her future community. The first ten members of her congregation were her own former high school students.

Motivation and Resources: Identification with the Crucified Jesus

In her talks and writings, Mother Teresa returns frequently to the message in Matthew's judgment scene: Christ identified with the poor, the hungry, the naked, the sick. These outcasts and outsiders resemble the crucified Jesus; service to them is service to Christ himself. Mother Teresa explains this very simply:

> Because we cannot see Christ, we cannot express our love to him in person. But our neighbor we can see and we can do for him or her what we would do for Jesus if he were visible.

The daily prayer she composed starts as follows:

Dearest Lord, may I see you today and every day in the person of your sick and whilst nursing them, minister unto you. Though you hide yourself behind the unattractive disguise of the irritable, the exacting, the unreasonable, may I still recognize you.

For Mother Teresa and her community, the principal means of identifying with the crucified Christ began with the Eucharist each morning. Jesus had invited his disciples to share his life when he took the cup at his Last Supper and said, "Drink from it, all of you; for this is my blood of the covenant which is poured out for many for the forgiveness of sins" (Mt 26:27). To share Jesus' cup meant to share his suffering and that of all the poor and afflicted with whom he was identified on the cross. This was the source of nourishment and strength for the difficult tasks the Sisters faced each day.

However, the Mass was by no means a ritual separated from life. Each day's activities were an extension of the Eucharistic union with Christ. Mother Teresa described it in this way, "In Holy Communion we have Christ under the appearance of bread. In our work we find him under the appearance of flesh and blood. It is the same Christ: 'I was hungry, I was thirsty, I was homeless.'" Mother Teresa expressed the continuity of the Mass with their work in these words, "We begin our day by seeing Christ in the consecrated bread, and throughout the day we continue to see him in the torn bodies of the poor. We pray, that is, through our work, performing it with Jesus, for Jesus and upon Jesus."

There is usually a mandatory wait of five years after death to begin the process of canonization. However, in December of 1997, Pope John Paul II waived this requirement in the case of Teresa of Calcutta.

Transformative Meditation
(See instructions in the Introduction)

Reading: Read slowly (out loud if possible) Matthew 25: 31-40, found on page 40-41.

Setting: A future judgment scene for which you now have the opportunity of obtaining choice reserved seats at the right hand side of the Son of Man. Jesus is presenting you a challenge as well as a vision of your future.

Guide: Imagine this *Son of Man* as portrayed by Matthew. He is not just a separate individual as the Risen Christ but merges with others as well. He is identified with all those unwanted, abandoned and suffering like himself. They share his cross. Listen as your *king* says to you at his right hand: "Come, you who are blessed by my father into the kingdom prepared for you from the foundation of the world." Feel surprised and joyful by this arrangement for you here and now. Then listen carefully to his requirements: *I was hungry and you gave me to eat, I was thirsty and you gave me something to drink.* Then looking toward the crucified Son of Man, notice that his extended arms embrace all the hungry oppressed people of the world especially the children. Include in this number some needy persons you know of. See them thirsting for needed water, food, clothing or shelter.

Listen further as Jesus continues, *I was a stranger and you took me in.* Now see his hands outstretched to all homeless people and millions of refugees throughout the world. Notice his special concern for children who have lost their parents. *I was naked and you gave me clothing.* Imagine his arms extended to those with insufficient clothing, those shivering in the cold or broiling in the hot sun during the day or unable to sleep at night without proper coverings. Think of particular people in need. *I was sick and you took care of me.* Visualize the crucified savior including all those who are sick and suffering, especially those most avoided and shunned, people with AIDS, leprosy or other diseases. See the Son of Man as sharing their sense of abandonment and loneliness. Recall particular people you may know personally or have heard about.

I was in prison and you visited me. Jesus himself suffered in prison and continues to be identified with millions of people in prisons throughout the world. Feel a sense of sorrow that our own country has one of the world's largest prison populations. Think especially of those who are in solitary confinement or tortured, those having no one who visits them, writes or phones.

Finally, identify with those on Jesus' right hand who are surprised and exclaim, "Lord when was it we saw you hungry and gave you food, or thirsty and gave you something to drink? And when was it that we saw you a stranger and welcomed you, or naked and gave you clothing? And when was it that we saw you sick or in prison and visited you?"

Listen carefully for Jesus' answer — one that will be extremely important for your future (and the world): "Truly, I tell you, just as you did it to one of the least of these who are my brothers and sisters, you did it to me" (25:40). Consider these words as a precious opportunity as well as a challenge to be included in that number in this scene. Jesus does not count the past and is ready to forgive. He is asking you to put aside worship of an unreal Christ separated from his beloved and suffering members. He is inviting you to turn instead to the real body of Christ which includes all the unwanted, avoided, abandoned, suffering, oppressed and poor of the world — especially people close to you right now. Take time to make that great decision with all your heart. When you do, listen again joyfully and gratefully to his words, "Come you blessed by my Father, inherit the kingdom prepared for you from the foundation of the world."

3   The Gospel of Luke

The Reality of the Risen Crucified Jesus

In his two volume work, the Gospel and Acts of the Apostles, Luke wishes to counter those who claimed that the Risen Jesus was not real and human. In the Acts of the Apostles, Luke cites Paul's final address to the presbyters of Ephesus. It is a strong warning to be vigilant about errors that may injure their flocks:

> Keep watch over yourselves and over all the flock, of which the Holy Spirit has made you overseers, to shepherd the church of God that he obtained with the blood of his own Son. I know that after I have gone, savage wolves will come in among you, not sparing the flock. Some even from your own group will come distorting the truth in order to entice the disciples to follow them. (20:28-30)

The errors are very serious and some of those listening to Paul may have been guilty of them: *some even from your own group.* Even though they are all shepherds and leaders, Paul calls some of them "savage wolves" remembering Jesus' words concerning wolves disguised in sheep's clothing. Such disciples are "distorting the truth." There are no particulars about these errors in the Acts of the Apostles. However there is a hint about their nature when Paul

51

states that the bishops are called to shepherd the flock of God that he obtained *with the blood* of his own Son. The mention of *blood* may emphasize Jesus' humanity.

If we follow up this hint in Luke's gospel, there will be good reason to believe that one of the errors above may be *docetism,* a belief or teaching that Jesus was only apparently human. Docetism implies that his death on the cross was only apparent and that visions of the risen Jesus lacked a real basis also. Such an error would affect the understanding of the "breaking of bread," celebrations of Jesus' Last Supper. An unreal Jesus would effectively attack the importance of this central Christian ritual.

To counter this serious error, Luke strongly emphasizes the humanity of Jesus both in the stories of Jesus' childhood and in the Passion narratives.

A Real Human Birth and Childhood

Luke carefully shows that Jesus did not swoop down from heaven in the guise of a human being, but was born like any other child. First of all Luke describes a definite historical setting: It is the time of the Roman Emperor Augustus when a census brings Mary and Joseph to register in Bethlehem after journeying from Nazareth in Galilee:

> He (Joseph) went to be registered with Mary, to whom he was engaged and who was expecting a child. While they were there, the time came for her to deliver her child. And she gave birth to her first born son and wrapped him in bands of cloth, and laid him in a manger, because there was no place for them in the inn. (2:5-7)

Luke emphasizes that this was a real human birth. After a nine month pregnancy, Mary delivered her first son and *wrapped him in bands of cloth.* This was a customary practice for every baby to keep their spines straight. Luke uses this detail as one of the signs to the shepherds: "This will be a sign for you: you will find a child *wrapped in bands of cloth* and lying in a manger" (2:12). Luke may be recalling the passage in the book of Wisdom where King Solomon describes himself as born like any other child, but he prayed and was given the gift of wisdom:

> When I was born, I breathed the common air and was laid on the earth that all people tread; and the first sound I uttered, as all do, was a cry; they wrapped me with *bands of cloths* and nursed me and cared for me. No king begins life in any other way.... Therefore I prayed, and prudence was given me; I called for help and there came to me a spirit of wisdom. (Ws 7:3-7)

This emphasis on Jesus' humanity continues when Luke describes the return of the family to Nazareth: "The child grew and became strong, filled with wisdom; and the favor of God was upon him" (2:80). Growth in outer and inner strength is a prime human characteristic. Jesus did not simply drop down from heaven. Luke has a similar statement when Jesus was twelve years old and returned to Nazareth with his parents from Jerusalem: "And Jesus increased in wisdom and in years, and in divine and human favor" (2:52).

The Wounds of Jesus: Signs of his Death and Humanity

Luke's resurrection story also emphasizes Jesus' humanity. The women came to anoint his body with spices. When they entered the tomb, "They did not find the *body*" (24:3). Only Luke specifically mentions the *body*, here and in 24:23 when the disciples on the way Emmaus relate to the mysterious stranger that "They did not find his *body* there." Luke also connects this with Jesus before his death by citing the angel's statement, "Remember how he told you, while he was still in Galilee, that the Son of Man must be handed over to sinners, and be crucified, and on the third day rise again" (24:6-7).

Luke's gospel moves toward its climax in the journey of two disciples from Jerusalem to Emmaus on Sunday, the third day after Jesus' death. They meet a mysterious stranger to whom they relate all that has been happening in Jerusalem that led to the crucifixion and death of Jesus along with the story of the women at the empty tomb. The stranger replies that they are slow of heart in believing the scriptures that the Messiah must suffer these things and then enter into his glory. When the disciples reach their destination at Emmaus, they ask the stranger to stay with them for the night. Later they recognize him as Jesus when he breaks bread with them:

> When he was at table with them, he took bread, blessed and broke it and gave it to them. Then their eyes were opened and they recognized him; and he vanished from their sight. (24:30-31)

The two disciples returned immediately to Jerusalem where they found the eleven gathered together. The two disciples then shared with them how they had recognized Jesus at the breaking of bread. Following this, Luke focuses our attention on the final vision of Jesus and his commission to his disciples:

> While they were talking about this, Jesus himself stood among them and said to them, "Peace be with you." They were startled and terrified and thought they were seeing a ghost. He said to them, "Why are you frightened, and why do doubts arise in your hearts? Look at my hands and my feet; see that it is I myself. Touch me and see; for a ghost does not have flesh and bones as you see that I have. (And when he had said this, he showed them his hands and his feet). [This last verse is not in some Greek manuscripts] (24:36-40)

It is not the face of Jesus that assures his human reality and recognition but his *hands and feet* mentioned twice. They are the place of the wounds that caused his death. The image that identifies him is that of the *crucified one.* In the next verse Luke mentions their joy and hesitancy in believing until Jesus asks for something to eat and takes a piece of broiled fish. Their joy could not have been from the sight of seeing the ugly disfigurement of his body but from seeing the wounds, now resplendent with divine glory in this luminous vision during the night.

At the very beginning of his gospel, Luke has taken great pains to present Jesus as truly human right from his birth and then on to his death and risen life. In that risen life, the image he emphasizes is that of the risen Lord with his five resplendent wounds. This is the same Christ whose presence is experienced in the breaking of bread. His wounds proclaim hope and forgiveness as the crucified one gives his final commission to his disciples:

> Thus it is written that the Messiah is to suffer and to rise from the dead on the third day, and that repentance and forgiveness of sins is to be proclaimed in his name to all nations, beginning from Jerusalem. (24:47)

"Jesus Remember Me When You Come Into Your Kingdom" (23:42)

There is extraordinary transforming power in calling upon the name of Jesus, the crucified one. This is especially evident in Luke's gospel. He writes,

> Two others also, who were *criminals* were led away to be put to death with him. When they came to the place that is called The Skull, they crucified Jesus there with the *criminals,* one on his right hand and one on his left. (23:33)

Only Luke uses this word "criminal" and repeats it three times: above and in 23:39 when he refers to "one of the criminals who were hanged there." Matthew and Mark call them "bandits." Perhaps they were revolutionaries inciting violence against Rome and supporting their cause with robberies. Luke uses the word "criminal" to stress how they represent people who commit the worst type of crimes. Jesus offers hope even to those who persist in evil up to the last moment of their lives. They might even have been murderers like Barabbas who was in prison awaiting execution (23:19).

Luke apparently distinguishes between people who look up *to* the cross with hope and the leaders and soldiers who looked up *at* the cross with disdain as they hurled their taunts at Jesus pinioned there:

> And the *people* stood by watching, but the *leaders* scoffed at him, saying, "He saved others; let him save himself if he is the Messiah, his chosen one!" The soldiers also mocked him, coming up and offering him sour wine, and saying, "If you are the King of the Jews, save yourself!" (23:36-37)

Mark and Matthew both note that even those crucified with Jesus increased his torment by also taunting him. Luke however notes the following:

> One of the criminals who were hanged there kept deriding him and saying, "Are you not the Messiah? Save yourself and us!" However the other one rebuked him, saying, "Do you not fear God, since you are under the same sentence of condemnation? And we indeed have been condemned justly, for we are getting what we deserve for our deeds, but this man has done nothing wrong." Then he said, "Jesus, remember me when you come into your kingdom." He replied, "Truly I tell you, today you will be with me in Paradise." (23:39-43)

Here Luke focuses on the power of calling upon the name of Jesus in the most desperate and impossible situation — that of a criminal in his last moments. The gospel invites everyone to take courage and experience Jesus' forgiving power. The gospel audience is actually made up of the *people* looking up to the cross in the story. They can have the same right to hope for instant forgiveness no matter what their lives have been. They are among those "who saw what had taken place, and returned home, beating their breasts" (23:48).

Immediately after these forgiving words of Jesus, Luke writes, "It was now about noon, and darkness came over the whole land until three in the afternoon, while the sun's light failed; and the curtain of the temple was torn in two." In the Acts of the Apostles, on Pentecost day, Peter addresses the crowds and speaks of the fulfillment of the prophecy of Joel, how on the last days, "The sun shall be turned to darkness and the moon to blood, before the coming of the Lord's great and glorious day. Then everyone who calls on the name of the Lord shall be saved" (2:20-21). We notice the similarity to the portents at Jesus' death where the sun's light fails. As in Acts, so also in Luke, calling on the name of the Lord brings salvation. The word *save* is pronounced by the leaders, the soldiers, and one of the criminals in a mocking sense. However, they are turned into reality by Jesus' words to the repentant criminal.

Actually the whole gospel points to this moment. At the beginning, the angel announces that the child's name will be Jesus — a name meaning God is a savior — even before he is conceived (1:31). At his circumcision, this name is emphasized once again. The transformative power present in this name will fully manifest itself at Jesus' death when the repentant criminal calls upon that name and is saved and forgiven.

In Luke's second volume, calling upon the *name* of Jesus is central to the life and prayer of believers. Miracles and healings take place when the name of Jesus is invoked. Peter, for example, tells a lame beggar, "In the name of Jesus Christ of Nazareth, stand up and walk" (3:6). And the man immediately begins to walk. When questioned, Peter announced to those present that "faith in his name" had made the beggar whole (3:16). Later, Peter testified to the Council that the man was standing in good health "by the name of Jesus Christ of Nazareth whom you crucified, whom God raised from the dead" (4:10). We note the connection to the cross when Peter speaks of Jesus, crucified and risen from the dead. Believers are soon known as "those who call upon the name of Jesus" (9:14, 21). Jesus' name also conveys the power of forgiveness. Peter tells Cornelius and Gentile believers, "All the prophets testify about him that everyone who believes in him receives forgiveness of sins through his name" (10:43). At baptism, believers, like Paul call upon his name (22:16).

It is significant that Jesus said to the good thief, "Today you will be with me in *Paradise*" (23:43).

This Greek word translates the Hebrew word for *Eden* (garden of) which means "pleasure." In this garden, according to the first chapters of Genesis, the devil (a later interpretation of the serpent) tempted humanity and won a victory. Luke has in mind that calling on the name of Jesus reverses this victory and reopens the closed garden for everyone. This may be one of the reasons Luke traces Jesus' ancestry back to Adam, (3:38) and not to Abraham as in Matthew. Immediately after this genealogy, we have the devil's temptation of Jesus who, unlike the first parents, resists the tempter. After this Luke notes that "when the devil had finished every test, he departed from him until an opportune time" (4:13). This time begins when "Satan entered into Judas" (22:3) to set in motion the events that lead to Jesus' death. At his arrest, Jesus said to his captors, "This is your hour, and the power of darkness" (22:53). Jesus' words on the cross imply a victory over the devil and a reversal of the path of humanity for all those who call upon him.

The Centurion and the Innocence of Jesus

In Matthew and Mark, the centurion proclaims that Jesus is God's son. However, Luke tells the story differently: "When the centurion saw what had taken place, he praised God and said, "Certainly this man was *innocent*" (23:47). This seems to be the sense of the Greek word, *dikaios*, in this context when we review what the converted criminal has just said: "We indeed have been condemned justly, for we are getting what we deserve for our deeds, but this man has done nothing wrong" (23:41).

Like Matthew and Mark, Luke is very concerned about the innocence of Jesus. In the Roman empire, it was dangerous to be a religious follower of a revolutionary leader. Three times Pilate says that he found no cause for punishment in Jesus' case. However, Luke seems to have in mind a deeper meaning also. A hint of this is found in the story of Philip and the conversion of an Ethiopian official in the Acts of the Apostles. Philip the Evangelist met this official who was returning in his chariot from worship in Jerusalem. He was reading the scriptures and Philip asked him if he understood what he was reading. He answered, "How can I unless someone guides me?" (8:31). So he invited Philip to ride in the chariot with him. The scripture passage was the following:

> Like a sheep he was led to the slaughter, and a lamb silent before its shearer, so he does not open his mouth. In his humiliation justice was denied him. Who can describe his generation? For his life is taken away from the earth. (Is 53:7-8)

The official then asked Philip, "About whom does the prophet say this, about himself or about someone else?" Then Philip began to speak, and starting from this passage, he proclaimed the good news about Jesus to him. The above scripture in its original context describes how faithful Israelites during the Babylonian exile patiently accepted their sufferings and offered them to God as a sacrifice in the name of all the people. Though they could no longer

offer holocausts in their destroyed temple, like uncomplaining innocent lambs going voluntarily to the altar of sacrifice, they offered
up their sufferings instead. They were like lambs that "had done
no violence, with no deceit in [their] mouth" (cf. 53:9).

Philip must have explained how Jesus was following the divine plan in scripture, offering his life voluntarily on the cross for
others without any kind of violent resistance. He was indeed a
Prince of peace. Peace is a central theme in Luke's gospel, beginning with the angels' proclamation of "peace on earth" at Jesus'
birth (2:14). This peace is not a cease-fire, but a proclamation of
love and reconciliation. While Matthew's Sermon on the Mount
asks us to pray for our enemies, Luke's version goes further by telling us to overcome past hurts by doing good to those who have
offended us. Jesus in Luke asks us even to bless those who curse us
(6:28). As an example, when there was an attempt to violently
defend Jesus at his arrest, he directly commands his disciples to
stop. Then he puts the peaceful message of the gospel into practice by restoring the ear of the high priest's servant that Peter had
cut off (22:50-51).

Consequently the centurion's statement about Jesus' innocence emphasizes the image of the wounded crucified Jesus as willingly suffering for others rather than using the violence and power
that his taunters under the cross demanded of him. They derided
him as weak and unable to save himself or others. However, he
was following God's plan that the weakness and nonviolence of
the cross was the way to save the world and bring true and lasting
peace.

Luke's Remembrance Theme — Especially of the Cross

More than Matthew and Mark, Luke highlights the importance of memory and remembrance. The mother of Jesus becomes
a model for this theme. She treasures the words of the shepherds
and ponders over them in her heart (2:19). A shadow of the cross

appears when Mary and Joseph present their child in the temple and Simeon says to Mary that her child will be a sign that will be opposed — and that "a sword will pierce your own heart" (2:35). This shadow continues when Jesus at twelve is lost three days in the temple, and Mary says to him afterward, "Child, why have you treated us like this? Look, your father and I have been searching for you in great anxiety?" He replied to them, "Why were you searching for me? Did you not know that I must be in my Father's house?" (2:49). These are Jesus' first words in the gospel and they mention his Father. They appear to be linked to Jesus' last words on the cross when he says, *"Father, into your hands I commend my spirit"* (23:46).

For Luke, *remembering* is especially centered about the cross. Jesus tells his disciples, "Let these words sink into you ears, 'The Son of Man is to be betrayed into human hands'" (9:44). Above all, Jesus specifically designs his Last Supper as a memorial feast, as a way to remember him:

> Then came the day of the Unleavened bread, on which the Passover lamb had to be sacrificed. So Jesus sent Peter and John, saying, "Go and prepare the Passover meal for us that we may eat it." (22:7)

In Luke there is a stronger connection between the sacrificed Passover lamb and Jesus' own Passover, where he will be the new lamb. Only in Luke does Jesus himself take the initiative by telling Peter and John to prepare the Passover (22:8). At table, he expresses to his disciples his deep longing to eat this meal with them: "I have eagerly desired to eat this Passover with you before I suffer." Again, this connection between his own suffering on the cross and Passover. Only in Luke, in the longer Greek text, can we find Jesus' command to continue celebrating this supper in his memory. However, it is found in the earlier account of the institution of the Supper found in the letters of Paul (1 Cor 11:23-26). In Paul, this "remembering" is found twice, once after the breaking of the bread and once after the sharing of the cup. The following is Luke's text:

> Then he took a loaf of bread, and when he had given
> thanks, he broke it and gave it to them, saying, "This is
> my body, which is given for you. Do this in remem-
> brance of me." And he did the same with the cup after
> the Supper, saying, "This cup that is poured out for you
> is the new covenant in my blood." (22:19-20)

Again the evangelist stresses the sacrificial nature of the supper by adding the words, "which is given for you." Both the bread/
body and the wine/blood proclaim that the event to be remembered is the sacrifice of Jesus crucified. The blood flowing from
his wounds is especially significant because this is the essential part
of the ritual of biblical sacrifice.

At the empty tomb, the divine messengers tell the women not
to look for Jesus, the living one, among the dead. They remind
them:

> *Remember* how he told you, while he was still in Gali-
> lee, that the Son of Man must be handed over to sin-
> ners, and be crucified, and on the third day rise again.
> (24:7)

Immediately following this, we have the words, "*Then they
remembered his words.*" The women have a privileged place, theirs
being the first to *remember* and thus begin the community Jesus
wished to establish. *The remembering* accomplishes several purposes:
First, that Jesus knew the path he was taking led to the cross; second, that it was in keeping with God's plan and not a horrible accident. The word *must* refers to a necessity inherent in the divine
plan. This necessity is also found in 24:26, 44-45 where the scriptures are specifically mentioned. Third, the memorial ritual estab-
lishes the way in which Jesus is to be remembered, and the image
to be recalled, namely, that of the risen and crucified one in God's
glory.

This remembering makes possible the continuity of Jesus' mission and his final words of commission:

> Then he opened their minds to understand the scriptures, and he said to them, "Thus it is written, that the Messiah is to suffer and to rise from the dead on the third day, and that repentance and forgiveness of sins is to be proclaimed in his name to all nations beginning from Jerusalem." (24:46-47)

The gospel now moves toward a triumphant ending. Jesus leads his followers toward Bethany where he lifts up his hands and blesses them. As he was blessing his loved ones, he withdrew from them and was carried into heaven. Luke has the gospel begin and end in a contrasting way. It begins in the temple where Zechariah the priest has a vision of the future. Meanwhile, "the whole assembly of the people was praying outside" (1:10). They were waiting for the priest to come out and give them the special priestly blessing. They began to wonder why he was delayed in doing so.

In contrast, at the end of the gospel, the risen Jesus, as priest through his sacrifice on the cross, gives the people the awaited blessing and then *they worshiped him.* This word is only used elsewhere in Luke regarding Anna's worship of God in the temple (2:38). We can only conclude that for Luke, to remember the crucified Jesus, is to remember God and worship him.

EXAMPLE: EDITH STEIN (1891-1942)

On October 10, 1998, Edith Stein was canonized a saint. Although a Christian convert, she freely sacrificed her life during the Holocaust rather than renounce her Jewish heritage. The following excerpts are taken from the homily of Pope John Paul II on that occasion:

Far be it from me to glory except in the Cross of our Lord Jesus Christ (Gal 6:14).

St. Paul's words to the Galatians, which we have just heard, are well suited to the human and spiritual experience of Teresa Benedicta of the Cross, who has been solemnly enrolled among the saints today. She too can repeat with the Apostle: "Far be it from me to glory except in the Cross of our Lord Jesus Christ."

The Cross of Christ! Ever blossoming, the tree of the Cross continues to bear new fruits of salvation. This is why believers look with confidence to the Cross, drawing from its mystery of love the courage and strength to walk faithfully in the footsteps of the crucified and risen Christ. Thus the message of the Cross has entered the hearts of so many men and women and changed their lives. The spiritual experience of Edith Stein is an eloquent example of this extraordinary interior renewal. A young woman in search of the truth has become a saint and martyr through the silent workings of divine grace: Teresa Benedicta of the Cross, who from heaven repeats to us today all the words that marked her life: *Far be it from me to glory except in the Cross of our Lord Jesus Christ!*

On 1 May 1987, during my Pastoral Visit to Germany, I had the joy of beatifying this generous witness to the faith in the city of Cologne. Today, 11 years later, here in Rome, in St. Peter's Square, I am able solemnly to present this eminent daughter of Israel and faithful daughter of the Church as a saint to the whole world. Today, as then, we bow to the memory of Edith Stein, proclaiming the indomitable witness she bore during her life and especially by her death. Now alongside Teresa of Avila and Thérèse of Lisieux, another Teresa takes her place among the host of saints who do honor to the Carmelite Order. Dear brothers and sisters who have gathered for this solemn celebration, let us give glory to God for what he has accomplished in Edith Stein.

We remember all concentration camp victims with respect.

Dear brothers and sisters! Because she was Jewish, Edith was taken with her sister Rosa and many other Catholic Jews from the Netherlands to the concentration camp in Auschwitz, where she died with them in the gas chambers. Today we remember them all with deep respect. A few days before her deportation, the woman religious had dismissed the question about a possible rescue: "Do not do it! Why should I be spared? Is it not right that I should gain no advantage from my Baptism? If I cannot share the lot of my brothers and sisters, my life, in a certain sense, is destroyed." From now on, as we celebrate the memory of this new saint from year to year, we must also remember the Shoah, that cruel plan to exterminate a people, a plan to which millions of our Jewish brothers and sisters fell victim. May the Lord let his face shine upon them and grant them peace (cf. Nb 6:25f.). For the love of God and man, once again I raise an anguished cry: May such criminal deeds never be repeated against any ethnic group, against any race, in any corner of this world! It is a cry to everyone: to all people of goodwill; to all who believe in the Just and Eternal God; to all who know they are joined to Christ, the Word of God made man. We must all stand together: human dignity is at stake. There is only one human family. The new saint also insisted on this: "Our love of neighbor is the measure of our love of God. For Christians and not only for them; no one is a stranger. The love of Christ knows no borders: Only the love of Christ makes us truly free."

Dear brothers and sisters! The love of Christ was the fire that inflamed the life of St. Teresa Benedicta of the Cross. Long before she realized it, she was caught by this fire. At the beginning she devoted herself to freedom. For a long time Edith Stein was a seeker. Her mind never tired of searching and her heart always yearned for hope. She traveled the arduous path of philosophy with passionate enthusiasm. Eventually she was rewarded: she seized the truth. Or better: she was seized by it. Then she discovered that truth had a name: Jesus Christ. From that moment on, the incarnate Word was her One and All. Looking back as a Carmelite on this period of her life, she wrote to a Benedictine nun: "Whoever seeks the truth is seeking God, whether consciously or unconsciously." Although Edith Stein had been brought up religiously by her Jewish mother, at the age of 14 she "had consciously and deliberately stopped praying." She wanted to rely exclusively on herself and was concerned to assert her freedom in making decisions about her life. At the end of a long journey, she came to the surprising realization: only those who commit themselves to the love of Christ become truly free.

This woman had to face the challenges of such a radically changing century as our own. Her experience is an example to us. The modern world boasts of the enticing door which says: everything is permitted. It ignores the narrow gate of discernment and renunciation. I am speaking especially to you, young Christians, particularly to the many altar servers who have come to Rome these days on pilgrimage: Pay attention! Your life is not an endless series of open doors! Listen to your heart! Do not stay on the surface, but go to the heart of things! And when the time is right, have the courage to decide! The Lord is waiting for you to put your freedom in his good hands.

St. Teresa Benedicta of the Cross was able to understand that the love of Christ and human freedom are intertwined, because love and truth have an intrinsic relationship. The quest for truth and its expression in love did not seem at odds to her; on the contrary she realized that they call for one another. In our time, truth is often mistaken for the opinion of the majority. In addition, there is a widespread belief that one should use the truth even against love or vice versa. But truth and love need each other. St. Teresa Benedicta is a witness to this. The "martyr for love" who gave her life for her friends, let no one surpass her in love. At the same time, with her whole being she sought the truth, of which she wrote: "No spiritual work comes into the world without great suffering. It always challenges the whole person." St. Teresa Benedicta of the Cross says to us all: "Do not accept anything as the truth if it lacks love. And do not accept anything as love which lacks truth! One without the other becomes a destructive lie."

The Mystery of the Cross gradually enveloped her whole life.

Finally, the new saint teaches us that love for Christ undergoes suffering. Whoever truly loves does not stop at the prospect of suffering: he accepts communion in suffering with the one he loves. Aware of what her Jewish origins implied, Edith Stein spoke eloquently about them: "Beneath the Cross I understood the destiny of God's People.... Indeed, today I know far better what it means to be the Lord's bride under the sign of the Cross. But since it is a mystery, it can never be understood by reason."

The mystery of the Cross gradually enveloped her whole life, spurring her to the point of making the supreme sacrifice. As a bride on the Cross, Sr. Teresa

Benedicta did not only write profound pages about the *Science of the Cross* (title of her book) but was thoroughly trained in the school of the Cross. Many of our contemporaries would like to silence the Cross. But nothing is more eloquent than the Cross when silenced! The true message of suffering is a lesson of love. Love makes suffering fruitful and suffering deepens love. Through the experience of the Cross, Edith Stein was able to open the way to a new encounter with the God of Abraham, Isaac and Jacob, the Father of our Lord Jesus Christ. Faith and the Cross proved inseparable to her. Having matured in the school of the Cross, she found the roots to which the tree of her own life was attached. She understood that it was very important for her "to be a daughter of the chosen people" and to belong to Christ not only spiritually, but also through blood. "God is spirit, and those who worship him must worship in spirit and truth" (Jn 4:24). Dear brothers and sisters, the divine Teacher spoke these words to the Samaritan woman at Jacob's well. What he gave his chance but attentive listener we also find in the life of Edith Stein, in her "ascent of Mount Carmel." The depth of the divine mystery became perceptible to her in the silence of contemplation. Gradually, throughout her life, as she grew in the knowledge of God, worshiping him in spirit and truth, she experienced ever more clearly her specific vocation to ascend the Cross with Christ, to embrace it with serenity and trust, to love it by following in the footsteps of her beloved Spouse.

St. Teresa Benedicta of the Cross is offered to us today as a model to inspire us and a protectress to call upon. We give thanks to God for this gift. May the new saint be an example to us in our commitment to serve freedom, in our search for the truth. May her witness constantly strengthen the bridge of mutual understanding between Jews and Christians. St. Teresa Benedicta of the Cross, pray for us! Amen.

Adapted from *L'Osservatore Romano*
Weekly Edition in English
14 October 1998

Transformative Meditation Exercise
(See instructions in the Introduction)

Introduction: The healing of memories can be one of the turning points of life. It can help us make a fresh new start by providing the means to free us from the prison of hurtful recollections and experiences. In this prison there is guilt and sorrow over people we may have hurt or offended at some time in the past. There are present also the painful wounds we have suffered from those who have hurt, injured or betrayed us.

Setting: Read slowly, and if possible aloud, the following story from the crucifixion scene in Luke 23:39:

> One of the criminals who were hanged there kept deriding him and saying, "Are you not the Messiah? Save yourself and us!" But the other rebuked him, saying, "Do you not fear God, since you are under the same condemnation? And we indeed have been condemned justly, for we are getting what we deserve for our deeds, but this man has done nothing wrong." Then he said, "Jesus, remember me when you come into your kingdom." He replied, "Truly I tell you, today you will be with me in Paradise."

(We have already seen in our study of Luke that the word, "criminal" is chosen to represent anyone — no matter how serious the offense may have been.)

Guide: Picture yourself as that "criminal" looking to Jesus on the cross. Gaze at the blood flowing from his wounds. Notice especially the blood flowing from his heart out through the wound in his side. Experience the love and compassion of Jesus "who has done nothing wrong," but is willing to suffer voluntarily out of love and compassion for you. As you do, allow his blood to wash and cleanse you from the hurtful memories that clog your heart. Repeat the words, "Jesus, remember me when you come into your kingdom."

To allow this cleansing and forgiving effect to continue, close your eyes and focus on your breath. On each intake, say the words, "Jesus remember me, when you come into your kingdom." Do this on at least ten slow breaths, using your fingers to count. Then listen to his reply, "This day you will be with me in Paradise." Repeat this likewise on ten breaths. With each breath experience deeper and deeper his love and compassion for any way you have hurt others (thinking all the while of specific cases). Finally let go of your wounds (to others) allowing them to be absorbed by Jesus' own wounds. Then send love and forgiveness to those who have wounded you in any way. Likewise, with each breath now say to yourself, "Lord remember *him/her* when your come into your kingdom" (ten times).

Finally let the memory of the loving wounds of the crucified Jesus take the place of all these old erased memories so you will not have a vacuum in your heart.

During the day, at the many odd moments that occur (e.g., traffic lights and jams!) use the "Jesus" prayer on each breath as often as you can. This means simply to say "Jesus" to yourself on each breath. Watch the transformation take place in your life as you repeat this exercise. As you expel the darkness of the old stereotypes and memories, you will find yourself slowing down your life, becoming more and more open to the beauty and love the exists in each person and in all of God's universe.

4   The Gospel of John

The Wounded Hands and Side of Jesus

Only John's Gospel describes the fifth wound in Jesus side. It was inflicted by a soldier who pierced Jesus with a spear in order to see if he were actually dead.

Also, only John's gospel specifically mentions the place of the *nails* on Jesus' hands.

The description of these wounds is found in the story of the doubting Thomas. It brings the gospel to its highest point in his confession that Jesus is Lord and God. Jesus' wounds were not incidental to this confession but actually made it possible. To explain this we will look at the three scenes about Thomas and the two levels of action that are taking place; first the surface level of Jesus' enemies and second, that of God's plan and power to transform the cruel wounds on the cross into instruments of love and salvation.

Three Gospel Scenes and Two Levels

The mutilated hands and side of the Risen Jesus, described only in John's gospel, appear in three scenes. Each scene emphasizes the contrast between believing and unbelieving that leads to the climactic confession of Thomas, "My Lord and My God" (20:28). Also, a double aspect to Jesus' wounds is apparent. Exteriorly the enemies of Jesus, the high priests (by way of plot) and the Roman soldiers (by way of execution) have made these wounds. On the surface they are an ugly disfiguration of a human body. Crucifixion, probably started by the Greeks, is possibly the most cruel type of death ever devised by human beings. Yet on another level one can also see as Thomas did, that Jesus' enemies have not disfigured Jesus but configured him as the new Paschal Lamb. These enemies have done this by unwittingly conforming to a hidden divine scriptural plan. The realization of this extraordinary contrast invites the listening audience to understand Thomas' confession and prompt them to make the same confession with him. The gospel has carefully led up to this moment and here we will trace the process.

1. The Double Level of the High Priest

After the raising of Lazarus, the chief priests and the Pharisees called a meeting to decide what they should do since Jesus was working so many miracles and threatening their authority. They feared that many people were following Jesus believing in him and that the Romans would come and destroy the temple and nation. Caiphas, the high priest for that year, said, "It is better for you to have one man die for the people than to have the whole nation destroyed" (11:48). The author comments further,

> He did not say this on his own, but being high priest that year he prophesied that Jesus was about to die for the nation, and not for the nation only but to gather into one the dispersed people of God. (11:51)

The evangelist is telling the gospel audience that the high priest was unaware of the significance of what he was saying. However, as an instrument of God because of his office, he was prophesying the priestly redemptive death of Jesus. After Caiphas' counsel, the chief priests made their plans to put Jesus to death. Thus they mysteriously act as priests to prepare a Passover sacrifice they never intended — that of Jesus' death on the cross. They sent out official orders that anyone knowing Jesus' whereabouts must inform them so an arrest can be made (11:57). The Pre-Passover purifications noted in John 11:55 hint at this double level: "Now the Passover of the Jews was near, and many went up from the country to Jerusalem to purify themselves." The author also reminds us about Caiphas' unwitting prediction about the nature of Jesus' death later on when Jesus is brought before the high priest for questioning: "Caiphas was the one who had advised the Jews that it was better to have one person die for the people" (18:14).

The Passover parallels continue in the gospel narrative after Jesus is brought from Caiphas to Pilate the Roman governor: "They themselves (the chief priests and leaders) did not enter the praetorium so as to avoid ritual defilement and to be able to eat the Passover" (18:28). When Pilate finds Jesus innocent, the priests and others cry out, "Crucify him" (19:6). Furthermore the Passover theme continues with the gospel note that it was the sixth hour (noon) of the preparation for the Passover, a time when the lambs were readied for slaughter (19:14). When Pilate asks, "Shall I crucify your king," the chief priests answer "yes" by stating, "We have no king but Caesar" (19:15). After this, the gospel states, "Then he (Pilate) handed him over to them to be crucified."

In summary, on one level, the chief priests are preparing for the Passover especially by bringing the lambs to sacrifice. On another level they are also leading Jesus to death not knowing they are fulfilling God's hidden plan to make Jesus the new Passover lamb.

2. The Double Level of the Soldiers

Likewise, Jesus' executioners unknowingly carry out the divine plan. The presence of soldiers (mentioned seven times) interlaces the passion account. It is they, along with Jesus (by way of non-resistance), who fulfill the scriptures.

> When the soldiers has crucified Jesus, they took his clothes and divided them into four parts, one for each soldier. They also took his tunic. Now the tunic was seamless, woven in one piece from the top. So they said to one another, "Let us not tear it, but cast lots for it to see who will get it." This was to *fulfill what the Scripture* says, "They divided my clothes among themselves and for my clothing they cast lots." (19:24)

As if to stress that the soldiers were unconsciously acting according to the divine plan, the author notes, "And that is what the soldiers did" (19:25). The scriptural references continue as Jesus is dying. After he speaks to his mother and beloved disciple by the cross the gospel continues, "After this, when Jesus knew that all was now finished, he said (in order to fulfill the scripture), "I am thirsty" (19:28). Then he accepts some wine and fulfills the passage from Psalm 69:21: "They gave me poison for food and for my thirst they gave me vinegar (sour wine) to drink."

An indirect Passover scriptural reference also exists in regard to the hyssop by which the wine was extended to Jesus on the cross:

> A jar full of sour wine was standing there. So they put a sponge full of the wine on a branch of hyssop and held it to his mouth. When Jesus had received the wine, he said, "It is finished." Then he bowed his head and gave up his spirit. (19:29-30)

The next passage refers to the first Passover when the Israelites were freed from a deadly plague and were able to leave Egypt. Moses instructed them,

> Go select lambs for your families, and slaughter the

Passover lamb. Take a bunch of hyssop, dip it in the blood that is in the basin, and touch the lintel and the two door posts with the blood in the basin. (Ex 12:22)

This sprinkling of blood on the Hebrew homes was a sign that they belonged to God and would be spared the plague suffered by the Egyptians. *Hyssop* is a plant that grows by the Nile river in Egypt. The use of this word at Jesus' death along with the dipping action from the jar OR basin is a reminder of the Passover nature of Jesus' death. The connection between the wine and Jesus' blood is strengthened when we keep in mind that a Semitic expression for wine is *the blood of the grape.* The bowl or jar of wine by the cross recalls the bowl of blood into which the hyssop was dipped to sprinkle blood on the homes of the Hebrews who were to be saved.

A further element in the divine plan is found when a soldier pierces Jesus' side with a lance:

Then the soldiers came and broke the legs of the first and of the other who had been crucified with him. But when they came to Jesus and saw that he was already dead, they did not break his legs. Instead, one of the soldiers pierced his side with a spear and at once blood and water came out. (19:32-34)

The fact that the soldiers broke the legs of the other crucified men but not those of Jesus is another reminder of the Passover ritual: "These things occurred that the scripture might be fulfilled, 'None of his bones shall be broken'" (19:36). This is part of the requirements for the Passover ritual that the lamb should be roasted entire, without any bones being broken (Ex 12:46).

There is also another indication of the double meaning of the Passover as referring both to Jesus' death as Passover lamb and the Passover lamb the Jewish priests were preparing for sacrifice. The expression *Preparation Day for the Passover* is repeated three times:

first as Pilate pronounces Jesus' sentence when the gospel notes that it was noon on this preparation day (19:14); second, when the leaders asked to speed the death of the crucified men by breaking their legs (19:31); third, at Jesus' burial: "And so, because it was the Jewish day of Preparation, and the tomb was nearby, they laid Jesus there" (19:42). All is in readiness for eating the Passover meal after sunset and for Jesus rising as the new Passover lamb in the next verse as the story of Jesus' resurrection begins.

The Fifth Wound: The Piercing of Jesus' Side and Its Significance

In the death of Jesus, the *piercing* wounds are central. They directly contribute to his death and have special meaning. This piercing is mentioned some 15 times in John counting the verb "crucify," the opening of Jesus' side and the repeated reference to nails, hands and side in the first resurrection appearances (20:20,25,27). The final words of the crucifixion account refer to this *piercing* as fulfilling the scriptures: "And again another passage of scripture says, 'They will look on the one whom they have pierced'" (19:37).

Effects of the Piercing Action

The text focuses on the fifth wound inflicted by a soldier who opens Jesus' side with a lance. Jesus was already dead but this was a supreme act of violation, cruelty and insensitivity. It caused heart-rending pain to those who loved Jesus most. This included his mother, the Beloved Disciple and Mary Magdalen. The writer gives close attention to this wound for a special reason: Just killing Jesus is not enough to make it appear as a sacrifice, like that of the Paschal lamb. The ritual of sacrifice requires that blood flow down to the ground. *So in the total plan of God this showed that God could reverse the cruel death and disgrace of Jesus' death by turning it into triumph. The flow of blood from Jesus' side became a redeeming sign of his death as the new Paschal lamb.*

This flow of blood from Jesus' side is closely linked to the sign of the lamb's blood in the first Passover described in Exodus, chapter 12. When a deadly plague threatened Egypt, God commanded Moses and Israel to select a Passover lamb and sacrifice it. To show which were the Hebrew homes to be spared from the plague, Moses instructed the elders to sprinkle blood over their doors and door posts, for God had said, "The *blood* shall be a *sign* for you, upon the houses where you are; and when I *see the blood,* I will pass over you…" (12:13). How crucial then for the Beloved Disciple to *see the blood* coming from Jesus' side. This was indeed the great Passover *sign: "He who saw* it has borne witness — his testimony is true — and he knows that he tells the truth, that you also may believe" (19:35). Then the evangelist adds the note that this was the fulfillment of the divine plan of scripture (19:36-37; cf. Zc 12:10).

That final scriptural quotation from the prophet Zechariah emphasizes both *piercing* and *seeing: "*They shall *look* on him whom they have *pierced"* (2:10). This quotation sums up the event that has already taken place. The mother of Jesus, Mary Magdalen and the Beloved Disciple have been standing by and looking on. They *saw* the water and blood come from Jesus' side and flow to the earth. The Beloved Disciple also represents the audience of believers of any time who look at the crucified Jesus and experience his presence, love and sacrificial forgiveness.

Considering the context of the prophet Zechariah's words it is striking how those who look upon the pierced one are themselves transformed:

> I will pour out a spirit of compassion and supplication
> on the house of David, so that when they look on the
> one whom they have pierced, they shall mourn for him,
> as one weeps over a firstborn.

And a few verses later,

On that day, a fountain shall be opened for the house
of David and the inhabitants of Jerusalem, to cleanse
them from sin and impurity. (13:1)

Another biblical reference strengthens the portrait of Jesus on
the cross as Paschal lamb. The soldiers unknowingly follow the
Passover ritual by not breaking Jesus' legs as they did those of the
other crucified men. According to ritual directions the sacrificial
lamb must be prepared with bones unbroken. This prompts the
gospel to note that Jesus' bones were not broken "so that the scripture might be fulfilled, 'none of his bones shall be broken'" (Ex
12:46).

The passion account concludes with the burial of Jesus as the
writer notes: "Because of the Jewish day of Preparation, as the tomb
was close at hand, they laid Jesus there" (19:42). Everything is now
ready for the Jewish Passover meal to take place. Yet at the inner
divine level, Jesus' enemies unwittingly made everything ready for
another Passover meal with Jesus as the new Paschal Lamb. Thus
we have an extraordinary divine reversal as God turns hostile actions into divine forgiveness and salvation.

The water from Jesus' side

The symbolism of water as representing the Spirit and connected with it runs throughout John's gospel. A culminating point
is Jesus' promise at the Feast of Tabernacles that he would be the
source of living waters to believers (7:38). [Or according to an al-
ternate Greek text, that the believers would be the source of the
Spirit for others.] This is followed by the author's note in the next
verse that Jesus was speaking of the Spirit which believers would
receive after his glorification. Other examples are the stories of
Nicodemus and that of the Samaritan Woman. Jesus told

Nicodemus, "No one can enter the Kingdom of God without being born of water and Spirit" (3:5). At the well of Samaria, Jesus told the woman, "The water that I will give will become in them a spring of water gushing up to eternal life" (4:14).

Application to The Final Three Scenes and Confession of Thomas (20:19-29)

Scene I. Jesus Appears to His Disciples on Sunday Evening (19-23). The opening atmosphere is one of fear, disarray and unbelief. The disciples have gathered together behind locked doors, fearing to be arrested also. However, Jesus suddenly appears in their midst and greets them. Then, "after he had said this, he showed them his hands and his side. The disciples then rejoiced when they saw the Lord." (To understand this transformation from the gospel audience's viewpoint, we must keep in mind all they have heard so far in the passion account, especially regarding the scriptures). The Passover parallels are the key to the interpretation. *The disciples rejoice because Jesus has also rejoiced in showing his pierced hands and side as transformed from his enemies' ugly mutilations into signs of the victorious Paschal Lamb.*

Such a transformation from hatred and disbelief to love and forgiveness can only be the amazing work of God. It proclaims the healing power of Jesus' wounds as a Paschal sacrifice and moves the disciples to a deeper level of believing. The words of Jesus, "Receive the Holy Spirit, whose sins you shall forgive..." complete the picture. John the Baptist had introduced Jesus as the "Lamb of God who takes away the sin of the world" (1:29). Through the cross, Jesus brought this prediction to completion. God's power turned the first level, that of the angry, unbelieving disfigurement of Jesus body, into a second level of forgiveness and belief.

Following this, Jesus shares what he has done with his disciples. He tells them, "As the Father has sent me, so I send you." Then he breathes upon them and says, "Receive the Holy Spirit

(Breath) of God." This is immediately applied to the forgiveness of sins, a power that is the supreme prerogative of God: "If you forgive the sins of any, they are forgiven them" (20:13). The passive voice (they are forgiven) means that *God* forgives (following the Semitic custom of indirect reference to God). Thus Jesus' words convey that believers can also act as God by being instruments of God's loving forgiveness to others.

By identifying themselves with Jesus as the lamb of God, his followers can likewise become forgiving lambs of God. This union with Christ is described in chapter six when Jesus speaks of *eating the flesh* of the Son of Man (6:53). The Passover background and parallels of this chapter help the audience recall the Passover ritual where God invites his people to "eat the flesh" of the Passover lamb (Ex 12:8). The eating of Jesus' bread in the Eucharistic meal is the way to become one body ("flesh" in John's gospel) with him.

Scene II. The other disciples tell Thomas (who had been absent), "We have seen the Lord." (Here the audience can identify with Thomas since they too must rely on the testimony of others). The disciples have not yet used the title, "Lord and God." This suggests that further reflection is necessary. Thomas, however, is still at the unbelieving level, and wants physical proof. Even today, the English dictionary defines a "doubting Thomas" as one who must see in order to believe.

Scene III. This takes place on the next Sunday, a week after Jesus appeared to the group of disciples. Thomas takes the risk to come to the community gathering. This suggests a change beginning to take place within him. Suddenly Jesus stands before him and says, "Put your finger here and see my hands, and bring your hand and put it into my side, and do not be unbelieving but believe." Thomas does not need to do this. This tells the gospel audience that mere tangible proof is not enough to move from the first level of unbelieving to the deeper level of believing. Instead, he exclaims, "My Lord and My God."

The evangelist does not explain how the change in Thomas, his supreme confession in Jesus' divinity, takes place. However the

Passover parallels again provide the key. At God's command, Moses lifts up his staff so that the waters of the sea fall back. The Egyptians follow in pursuit, but the waters flow back causing them to drown in the sea. With this final sign, "the people feared the LORD and believed in the LORD and in his servant Moses" (Ex 14:31). God's saving intervention is repeated throughout the Exodus story: "that the people and Egypt may believe that I am the Lord (Yahweh)" (Ex 14:4,18).

The above process was summarized in the gospel prologue with Jesus' description as the eternal Word of God: "In the beginning was the Word." This Word only became completely external and evident through Jesus' piercing on the cross and his subsequent transforming resurrection. This extraordinary event was predicted in the gospel when Jesus said, "When you have lifted up the son of Man, then you will know that I AM" (8:28). Other I AM statements of Jesus cloak his divinity, a reality that will become fully recognized through the cross and its transforming power.

This great divine reversal only takes place when the terrible wounds of hate on Jesus' body through his enemies become transformed into glorious, joyful signs of forgiveness. Only God can make such a transformation and transfer this power to others. This is what Thomas recognized. Yet it only happened because Jesus intervened to call and invite him to do so.

Transformative Meditation
(See guide in the Introduction)

Introductory note: Meditating on the side/ heart of Jesus has been a very fruitful source of energy and transforming love for many mystics. God made the following "impossible" promise of a mystical heart transplant operation over two thousand five hundred years ago through the prophet Ezekiel 36:26-27:

"A new heart I will give you and a new spirit I will put within you; and I will remove from your body the heart of stone and give you a heart of flesh."

This passage has been read for many centuries in the liturgy of the central feast in Judaism each year, *Yom Kippur,* the Day of Atonement. It proclaims that God has the power to forgive and change even the stoniest of hearts and create new hearts filled with the Spirit and love. Jesus' death parallels the day of Atonement in offering this new heart to everyone. This is why all the gospels point out the personal changes that take place in people after Jesus' death. In Matthew, Mark and Luke this is exemplified in the conversion of the centurion or the repentance (in Luke) of one of the "criminals" crucified with Jesus. In John, it is the change that takes place in Thomas. So the "heart transplant" text in Ezekiel has a long tradition of power when used in meditation.

Biblical Text: Read (aloud if possible) the above short text from Ezekiel and repeat it to yourself until you have it memorized.

Setting: Imagine yourself in the company of the Mother of Jesus, Mary Magdalen and the Beloved Disciple at the foot of the cross. With them you look up at the crucified Jesus. You share with them their agonizing shock when one of the soldiers pierces Jesus' side with a lance. You witness this horrible desecration of his body and observe the water and blood flowing from his heart to the ground. You ask God fervently to open your own heart to experience the love that prompted Jesus to give his life for you and all humanity.

Begin thinking of Jesus' unique love for his mother Mary and his father Joseph. Then imagine his heart expanding to include the love of all children toward their parents and all parents toward their children. Breathe this love in deeply several times and experience it as much as you can. Next, imagine Jesus' special love for his closest friends — for Mary Magdalen who stood by him when others deserted him, for Peter even after he denied three times under oath that he even knew Jesus, for Judas who betrayed him to the authorities. Then picture the heart of Jesus expanding further to include all the beautiful love of friends for each other and all the affection between lovers. Breathe this love in and out several times. Next consider inwardly the compassionate love of Jesus for all the sick who came to him whether they were lepers, diseased, disabled or in mental anguish. Now see the heart of Jesus expanding to include the love of all care-givers, doctors and nurses in hospitals and homes as they minister to the sick. Come close to Jesus' heart and breathe this love in and out.

Finally, imagine that generous heart expanding until it becomes the one great throbbing heart of the Universe, the eternal Word and Expression of God. Compare this to the littleness of your own heart and love. Now recall the astounding promise of Ezekiel that God's power can effect the miracle of a heart transplant. Repeat Ezekiel's words to yourself. Believe that God can really change your own "heart of stone" into a "heart of flesh," the compassionate and sensitive heart of Jesus. Ask that your heart may become one with Jesus in his great loving compassion.

Now open yourself to receive this great transplant and watch Jesus as he does it. He says to you, as at the Last Supper, "Take and eat (this bread); this is my body." This is the total gift of himself with its center as the great throbbing and loving heart of the Universe. Receive this heart, the greatest gift in the world, into your inmost being. For a moment, stop and experience the love that this heart brings. Rejoice and be grateful for it. Then call to mind people who especially need of something from you; send them your love, energy or forgiveness, if needed. Breathe this compassionate love out to them as you imagine their faces.

What you are doing is actually something you may have learned as a little child under another name: You are making a "Spiritual Communion". This grace of a spiritual communion with Jesus and others is always available. This meditation is one way to go about it. Essentially it is rooted in a great desire to experience this loving change and believing it can happen.

EXAMPLE: DOROTHY DAY (1897-1980)

In John's gospel, Pilate asked Jesus, "Are you a king?" Jesus replied, "For this I was born, and for this I came into this world, to testify to the truth. Everyone who belongs to the truth hears my voice" (18:37). Dorothy's entire life was a daily, often stormy search for the truth, putting love into practice and finally communicating it to others.

Her father, John Day, was a journalist. This must have influenced Dorothy's lifelong interest in reporting, writing and publishing. After spending two years at the University of Illinois, she left college at nineteen and worked for a socialist newspaper. A year later in 1917, she joined a women's march on Washington for voting rights. A disappointing marriage in 1920 lasted only one year. After moving to Chicago, she became active in the Communist *International Workers of the World*. She was jailed for her involvement in the "red raids" of that time. Anyone suspected of Communist ties was at the risk of being jailed.

Her brief time in jail affected her profoundly as she associated with the dejected, suffering people of the street she met there. She read the bible while in prison but was not attracted to any "organized religion." After her release from jail she went to Chicago. While there she wrote a popular book entitled, *The Eleventh Virgin.* Later in life she was ashamed of this expose of her stormy youth including her tragic romance, abortion, brief marriage, travels and social involvement. She tried to seize whatever copies she could lay hold of.

In 1925 she entered a "common-law marriage" in New York with Foster Batterham, a dedicated biologist, environmentalist and atheist. They had a child, Tamar Teresa, in 1927. Dorothy had their child baptized in the Catholic church and began studying to be a Catholic. This was simply too much for Foster and he separated from her. This was during the time of the Great Depression. Dorothy was deeply disturbed to see thousands of hungry people walking the streets looking for work. In December, 1932, she took part in the hunger march on Washington D.C. In her writings she supported the causes of the poor. Among these were many articles for the liberal Catholic magazine, *Commonweal.*

Actually, Dorothy's real conversion began with her association with Peter Maurin who had come from France after being active there in organizing workers. His vision of the future was a world where families could live in small communities close to the earth and be self-sustaining. He also felt there was a critical need for "houses of hospitality" where the poor and hungry could be served in a person-to-person family setting. These houses would offer food, shelter, clothing and job training for employment.

Dorothy Day and Peter Maurin decided to work together. They started with a monthly newspaper, *The Catholic Worker,* to publicize their ideas. It first saw light on Mayday, 1933 with 2500 copies paid for by $57.00 in gifts from their friends. Within a few years the publication reached 150,000. Each issue sold then, as it still does, for "a penny a copy." Many copies are distributed free of charge. Up to the present day, The *Catholic Worker* continues to spread the original vision of Peter Maurin and Dorothy Day with its interesting articles, book reviews and news from widely scattered hospitality houses. Some of these houses publish their own newsletters as well.

As interest and support increased, Dorothy and Peter rented a store in New York City. Gradually other houses of hospitality sprang up across America. Thousands of volunteers then and now continue the spirit and service enthusiasm of the Catholic Worker. From 1933 until her death in 1980, Dorothy lived in a Catholic Worker house, edited the newspaper, served meals to the hungry and traveled all over the U.S. founding new houses and encouraging already established ones. At the same time she made her voice heard in the events of the outside world.

She took a firm stand against Franco when he started a civil war in Spain, even though he was widely supported by the church. This alienated her from a good many Catholics. In addition, she lost many friends when she called for pacifism in trying to prevent

World War II. In her 60's she was riding buses in the South for civil rights or marching on the west coast with Cesar Chavez to support farm workers. Some of her stands on peace were very unpopular with the Catholic hierarchy. The Archdiocese of New York even asked her (unsuccessfully) to take the word "Catholic" from the *Catholic Worker* title since its views did not necessarily correspond with "official views."

While Dorothy was very devoted to the church and the sacraments, she did not hesitate to speak out on social issues when she felt that church leaders did not act or speak according to her understanding of the gospel. On one occasion in 1949, the grave diggers at Calvary Cemetery in New York went on strike for better wages against their church employers. Cardinal Spellman refused to negotiate and asked seminarians to volunteer to take the workers' places in digging graves. Dorothy and many Catholic Workers went to the cemetery gates and joined the picket line with the workers.

According to Dorothy's memoirs, she never had extraordinary visions or revelations. Each day she struggled against pride; the effort to serve others with humility was her *passion*. She meditated on Jesus' crucifixion throughout her life. "Taking up the cross" meant forgetting herself and serving others with humility. When she failed, she would humbly ask God and others for pardon. Each day she longed for time to be quiet, to read, and to pray, but her life was one interruption after another. She accepted this and surrendered to what each day brought her. She regarded the hospitality houses not as an adjunct to her life but as her own cherished "family in Christ." She never "retired" from this work but continued on for 50 years until she died at age 83.

5   The Letters of Paul

"I have Been Crucified with Christ" (Galatians 2:20)

The letters of Paul include the earliest known Christian literature. They were written from about 50 to perhaps the early 60's AD. For this reason alone they are a most valuable witness to early Christian beliefs. To a large extent, western Christianity owes its origins to the work of this zealous, indefatigable apostle who journeyed through the Roman Mediterranean world establishing new communities while encouraging and visiting older ones. If asked the reason for his extraordinary success, he would respond by saying he owed it to his union with the risen crucified Christ whose power worked through him. We know about his theology and motivation primarily through his letters in so far as they answered questions addressed to him. Otherwise we have no orderly summary of his thought. The best we can do is to study his letters with as much knowledge of their context as possible. We will only touch those letters which reveal most about Paul's relationship to the cross.

The Letter to the Galatians

Paul was a founder of Christian communities who deliberately left the completion of his work to others in order to concentrate on starting new communities. Sometimes he had to leave a community earlier than he had planned due to troubles in previous places. His success with non-Jews was largely due to his preaching of religious freedom from religious laws especially those bound up in his own Jewish background. Such laws dealt with foods, ritual, feasts and requirements drawn from the bible and amplified through centuries of tradition. He did not object if Jewish Christians wished to keep these practices. However, he felt that even though he had been a Jewish rabbi himself, he could not impose Jewish ritual requirements on Gentiles. He preached that faith in Christ was sufficient for non-Jews and nothing need be added.

At the same time, there were other Christian preachers who disagreed with him. They claimed that Christ did not come to do away with these Jewish laws which were all from God. After all, Moses, Abraham and others had been circumcised and kept these requirements; subsequent generations, therefore, should do likewise. It was fine for Gentiles to become Christians, but like Jesus they should become Jews, at least in the minimal sense. When Paul had to leave his new fervent Christian communities, they did not have the gospels or other writings to guide them — such did not yet exist. They only had oral teachings about Jesus and of course the Hebrew bible. Often, visiting Christian preachers from other places came to teach them. They sometimes claimed that Paul had given them "a short course," but now they could become "perfect" by keeping all the biblical laws. For Gentiles, they advised at least circumcision and observance of the basic Jewish food laws.

These visiting teachers had considerable influence. Paul was so alarmed when he received the news, that he wrote his most vehement and scathing letter — the letter to the Galatians. Paul was afraid that any added Jewish requirements would give the impression that the cross of Christ was not really enough and that more was needed. This in effect would nullify what Christ has done. We cannot go through his whole letter, but will limit ourselves to Paul's emphasis on the cross.

First of all, Paul had to show that his teaching was based on an independent revelation of the risen crucified Christ. He wrote that God... "was pleased to reveal his Son to me" (1:15) so he did not feel obliged to confer with other Christian leaders, with the exception of a two week visit to Peter and James three years after his conversion and again after he had been a Christian for over fourteen years (1:18-2:1). These "pillars" of the church approved his work and type of preaching among the Gentiles. However a snag came when Peter visited Galatia and began to eat only with Jewish Christians in order to observe the food regulations of the Jewish Law. Despite Peter's actions, Paul refused to change his views that only faith in Christ was required for Gentile believers. He wrote that he "died to the law" when he became a convert so that he might live for God (2:19). The new center of his life became union with the crucified risen Christ:

> I have been crucified with Christ; and it is no longer I who live but it is Christ who lives in me. And the life that I now live in the flesh I live by faith in the Son of God who loved me and gave himself for me. (2:20)

What impels Paul in his teaching and lifestyle is the image of Christ wounded and crucified as a sign of the loving gift of himself. Paul states that if something had to be added to this by way of obligation, then "Christ died for nothing" (2:21). What Paul has personally experienced is what he preached. He seems carried away by emotion as he writes,

> You foolish Galatians! Who has bewitched you? It was before your eyes that Jesus Christ was publicly exhibited as crucified. (3:1-2)

With a touch of humor in those words, Paul writes that someone must have put the Galatians under a magic spell with such contrary teachings. After all, he had publicly preached the image of a Christ nailed to the cross. Actually Paul had never seen the earthly Christ, nor had his audience. Nevertheless, this was the only way that he identified Jesus — as the crucified one. Paul pictures Christ as becoming an object of curse on the cross to separate people from the curse of obligatory religious laws:

> Christ redeemed us from the curse of the law by becom-
> ing a curse for us — as it is written, "Cursed is every-
> one who hangs on a tree." (3:13)

In the above text we see that Paul well appreciated the disgrace and ignominy of the cross that made Jesus an object of curse
according to Deuteronomy 21:23. Jesus took this on himself so
believers would be free from the curse of obligatory past religious
obligations. According to Paul, believers are so closely united to
Jesus that he says of them that they have been "clothed in Christ"
through the waters of baptism (3:27). This makes them free from
all the walls dividing humanity.

> There is no longer Jew or Greek, there is no longer slave
> or free, there is no longer male and female; for all of you
> are one in Christ Jesus. (3:28)

While Paul is opposed to the slavery of following the law, he
is also against the slavery of so-called "freedom":

> For you were called to freedom, brothers and sisters;
> only do not use your freedom as an opportunity for self-
> indulgence, but through love become slaves of one an-
> other. For the whole law is summed up in a single com-
> mandment, "You shall love your neighbor as yourself."
> (5:13-14)

Again the apostle presents the imagery of the crucified Jesus
to motivate Christians to put aside selfishness and excessive indi-
vidualism: "Those who belong to Christ Jesus have crucified the
flesh with its passions and desires. If we live by the Spirit, let us be
guided by the Spirit" (5:24-25).

Since ancient professional scribes ordinarily wrote the actual
letters which were only signed by their authors, Paul closes his letter in an unusual way. In contrast to the finer hand of the scribe
who wrote the letter up to this point, he inscribed this last part in

his own hand and with large letters for greater emphasis: "SEE WHAT LARGE LETTERS I AM WRITING WITH MY OWN HAND" (6:11). He is troubled by his opponents' boasting that they have won over some of his converts and persuaded them to be circumcised as well as to observe other Hebrew biblical laws. In contrast, Paul declares, "May I never boast of anything except the cross of our Lord Jesus Christ by which the world has been crucified to me and I to the world" (6:14).

As for boasting about such external physical signs, Paul closes with these fiery words: "From now on, let no one make trouble for me: for I carry the marks of Jesus branded on my body." These marks on Paul's body duplicate Jesus' wounds and sufferings through the floggings and punishment Paul received from civil authorities during his journeys. In the Greek text, the word for "marks" is *stigmata*. Because of this, the word was later used to refer to the visible signs of Jesus' wounds on the hands, feet and side that certain believers such as St. Francis of Assisi received from God.

(The Letter to the Romans will not be discussed because it simply builds on and amplifies the teaching on the cross found in Galatians.)

The First Letter to the Corinthians

Corinth, one of the largest cities of the Roman Empire, was a great center of business, learning, religion, culture and entertainment. Most shipping and business from east to west stopped at Corinth. This was because Corinth was located at the western side of a narrow seven mile wide isthmus between northern and southern Greece. Ships in ancient times did not like to sail outside the sight of shore. The more direct route to Rome across the open stretch of the Mediterranean was dangerous. Consequently, ships arrived at the eastern end port of Cenchrae where merchandise was brought overland to another ship at Corinth. It was also possible to transport the entire small ship overland, perhaps on rails to the other side of the isthmus and then proceed on to Italy.

In the Roman Empire, Corinth became a by-word for a place you simply must visit some time in your life. The Greek language even had expressions which emphasized this. To refer to someone as a "real Corinthian" meant that they were sharp business persons; to "corinthize" meant to live it up and enjoy life to the full; to say that a woman was "a Corinthian girl" was by no means complimentary. Corinth was an important religious center as well. The great temple of Aphrodite, before the time of Paul, was one of the wonders of the world. "Devout" sailors looked forward to visiting Corinth and enjoying the company of the many "sacred prostitutes" who represented the popular goddess of love and fertility.

For Paul, this city represented a great challenge to his missionary zeal. He wrote to them later, "I came to you in weakness and in fear and in much trembling" (2:3). One of the first problems Paul faces in this letter is how to offset the prestige of "wisdom" and its teachers among the Greeks. For them, philosophy was far more than an academic endeavor; it was an entire way of living. The custom was to find a teacher whom you could follow, study and imitate. A matter of great prestige was to have a well-known teacher. Many Christian Greek converts regarded their faith as a wisdom school and attached themselves to this or that teacher with great pride.

When Paul heard of this, he was completely shocked. It was diametrically opposed to the spirit of the crucified savior at the center of his life and preaching. He wrote to the Corinthians:

> I appeal to you brothers and sisters by the name of our Lord Jesus Christ that all of you be in agreement and that there be no divisions among you... for it has been reported to me by Chloe's people that there are quarrels among you... what I mean is that each of you says, "I belong to Paul," or "I belong to Apollos," or "I belong to Cephas (Peter)" (1:10-12).

Paul minces no words in answering, "Was Paul crucified for you? Or were you baptized in the name of Paul?" There is simply no place for pure human discipleship in their lives since they belong directly to the crucified Christ. For this reason Christ sent him to "proclaim the gospel, and not eloquent wisdom, so that the cross of Christ might not be emptied of its power" (1:17). Then Paul announces a central theme of his letter: "The message about the cross is foolishness to those who are perishing, but to us who are being saved it is the power of God."

God's saving plan upsets all human plans and expectations: "For Jews demand signs and Greeks desire wisdom, but we proclaim *Christ crucified,* a stumbling block to Jews and foolishness to the Gentiles." To those who are being saved this crucified Christ "is the power and wisdom of God" (1:22-25). As proof of this, Paul asks them to consider their own call. Were they called to faith because they were powerful, noble, or wise philosophers? On the contrary, "God chose what is low and despised in the world... so that no one might boast in the presence of God" (1:29).

The same contrast was true of Paul's arrival and preaching in Corinth:

> When I came to you, brothers and sisters, I did not come proclaiming the mystery of God to you in lofty words or wisdom. For I determined to know nothing among you *except Jesus Christ, and him crucified.* (1 Cor 2:1-2)

It did not matter that Paul came to them "in weakness and in fear and in much trembling" (2:3). On the contrary it showed that the gospel he preached had its success not from any human source but from the power of God. This infinite divine source is an impenetrable secret; human beings and even the rebellious angels led by Satan cannot understand weakness and the renunciation of power:

> We speak God's wisdom, secret and hidden, which God decreed before the ages for our glory. None of the rulers of this age understood this; for if they had they would not have crucified the Lord of glory. (2:7-8)

This last sentence, "None of the rulers, etc...." is one of Paul's great gems. Renouncing power and control is so completely foreign to human ways that nothing can withstand God's power which comes through the weakness of the cross.

Paul applies this wisdom to his own preaching and apostolate. He is willing to be considered a fool and spectacle because it opens the way for God's power and grace to work:

> For I think that God has exhibited us apostles as last of all, as men sentenced to death, because we have become a spectacle to the world, to angels and to mortals. We are fools for the sake of Christ, but you are wise in Christ. We are weak, but you are strong. You are held in honor, but we in disrepute. (4:9-10)

The Last Supper as a Proclamation of the Cross

Paul's appreciation of the mystery of God's reversal of human values in the cross brings him special insights into the meaning of the celebration of the Lord's supper.

When Paul's words were read to the community, they must have been shocked. They continue to shock us today by their directness:

> Now in the following instructions I do not commend you, because when you come together it is not for the better but for the worse. For to begin with, when you come together as a church there are divisions among you and to some extent I believe it. (11:17-18)

In the early church, the Corinthian community shared a meal together when they celebrated the Lord's supper. They brought food and drink from their homes to the meeting place. However, those who were richer or of higher social class tended to eat in small groups with those of similar background. Consequently their food and drink was more abundant and of better quality. Paul is deeply concerned that this situation does not reflect the values of the crucified Christ. This segregated Eucharist does not embody a sincere love for the poor or less privileged. So Paul asks them, "Do you not have homes to eat drink in? Or do you show contempt for the church of God and humiliate those who have nothing?" (11:22).

In proof, Paul then cites the tradition he has received about Jesus' Last Supper:

> The Lord Jesus, on the night he was betrayed took a loaf of bread, and when he had given thanks, he broke it and said, "This is my body that is for you. Do this in remembrance of me. In the same way, he took the cup also, after supper, saying, "This cup is the new covenant in my blood. Do this as often as you drink it, in remembrance of me." (11:23-26)

Paul then continues, "For as often as you eat this bread, and drink the cup, you proclaim the Lord's death." This proclamation refers to the meaning of his death as expressed in the institution story. Jesus dies out of love for others: a *body that is for you* and a cup that is his blood poured out for others. Consequently, if the Corinthians during the meal are shaming the poor by not sharing freely, it cannot be a proclamation of Jesus' love for others. In fact, their ritual would be a matter for judgment and punishment: "Whoever, therefore, eats the bread or drinks the cup of the Lord in an unworthy manner will be answerable for the body and blood of the Lord" (11:27).

The Second Letter to the Corinthians

There was a long period between the first and second letter to Corinth. During this time, Paul experienced several serious crises. One of these was severe persecution at Ephesus that caused him acute suffering and even threatened his life. He introduces his letter by blessing God "who consoles us in all our affliction, so that we may be able to console those who are in any affliction" (1:3). He continues by describing what happened to him and his companions at Ephesus: "We do not want you to be unaware, brothers and sisters, of the affliction we experienced in Asia (Roman Province of Asia); for we were so utterly, unbearably crushed that we despaired of life itself." In fact, Paul had been for a time in prison awaiting a death sentence: "Indeed, we felt that we had received the sentence of death so that we would rely not on ourselves but on God who raises the dead" (1:8-9).

A second crisis occurred sometime between the two letters. In a visit he had evidently made to Corinth, Paul was rejected by a group of Corinthian Christians. This is why he writes, "I made up my mind not to make you another painful visit" (2:1). As a result, he wrote them instead a letter with much "distress and anguish of heart and with many tears" (2:3). In this letter he asked the Corinthians to repent for what they had done to him and punish the leader who personally opposed him.

These painful crises and suffering prompted Paul to meditate more deeply on the meaning and value of the cross in his personal life. He came to realize that "the sufferings of Christ" were not apart from himself, but in his own life as he experienced the same things Jesus did. Also he understood that this conformity to the cross had a precious value in sharing and extending the redemptive meaning of the cross in regard to others:

> For just as the sufferings of Christ are abundant for us,
> so our consolation is abundant through Christ. If we
> are being afflicted, it is for your consolation and salvation. (1:5-6)

This leads him to the tremendous new insight that their own bodies are a living cross proclaiming the meaning of Christ's mission. Paul is filled with new confidence despite apparent failures. The best preaching of the cross has been the very sufferings they have endured. These sufferings have been transformed into an effective part of Christ's redemptive action for others:

> We are afflicted in every way, but not crushed; perplexed, but not driven to despair; persecuted, but not forsaken; struck down but not destroyed; always carrying in our body the death of Jesus, so that the life of Jesus may also be made visible in our bodies. For while we live, we are always being given up to death for Jesus' sake so that the life of Jesus may be made visible in our mortal flesh. So death is at work in us, but life in you. (4:8-12).

As for defending himself against his opponents, Paul does not want to descend to their level by boasting about his accomplishments. However, they have forced him to set forth the truth, even though he must speak "as a fool" (11:23). If he must compete with his persecutors, Paul will only count the sufferings and disgrace he endured as an apostle:

> Are they ministers of Christ? I am talking like a madman — I am a better one: with far greater labors, far more imprisonments, with countless floggings, and often near death. (11:23)

Then follows a long list of these sufferings which makes one wonder how a human being could endure so much. At the end, he says, "If I must boast, I will boast of the things that show my weakness" (11:30). At the end Paul illustrates this with a story that seems at first far less amazing than his previous list:

> In Damascus, the governor under King Aretas guarded the city of Damascus in order to seize me, but I was let down in a basket through a window in the wall, and escaped from his hands. (11:32-33)

Considering how important *honor* was for people of the time we will better understand why Paul tells this story in detail rather than accounts of three shipwrecks at sea, his five floggings of 39 lashes each from the Jews (40 was the law, but 39 was the practice in order to not approach the limit!). Or his being beaten innumerable times by non-Jewish authorities. Tradition tells us that Paul was of small stature. So the rather humorous feat of stuffing him into a basket in order to escape is rather embarrassing!

Paul's adversaries boasted of visions and revelations, so he is forced to "act the fool" and tell about his own mystical experiences. However, lest the greatness of his revelations inflate him too much, he admits that he had some unnamed humiliating affliction (perhaps affecting his personal appearance):

> A thorn was given me in the flesh, a messenger of Satan to torment me, to keep me from being too elated. Three times I appealed to the Lord about this, that it would leave me, but he said to me, "My grace is sufficient for you, for power is made perfect in weakness." (12:7-9)

For Paul, all his success was not because he relied on special human strength, talents or gifts, but was only due to God's power and grace. He had become a living cross witnessing how God works through the least likely human instruments. Thus he concludes:

> So I will boast all the more gladly of my weaknesses, so the power of Christ may dwell in me. Therefore I am content with weaknesses, insults, hardships, persecutions, and calamities for the sake of Christ; for whenever I am weak, then I am strong. (12:11)

Transformational Meditation: Philippians 2:3-11
(See Instructions in the Introduction)

Background: Paul writes this letter from prison, fearing it may be his last. He sent it to his beloved community in Philippi, Greece. Having heard from them in a recent letter he realizes there have been some sharp disagreements, bad feelings and arguments among them. He responds to this situation by quoting an ancient Christian song. This hymn portrays the entire life of Christ as a passion that culminated in the cross. This suffering consisted in his continued "emptying" of himself in order to serve others. This was a favorite passage for Dorothy Day to help her consider her whole life with its daily interruptions as a challenge to overcoming pride and self-centeredness.

Text: Do nothing from selfish ambition or conceit, but in humility regard others as better than yourselves. Let each of you look not to your own interests, but to the interests of others. Let the same mind be in you that was in Christ Jesus,

> Who though he was in the form of God
> did not regard equality with God
> as something to be exploited,
> but emptied himself,
> taking the form of a slave,
> being born in human likeness.
> And being found in human form,
> he humbled himself
> and became obedient to the point of death —
> even death on a cross.
>
> Therefore God exalted him
> and gave him the name
> that is above every name,
> so that at the name of Jesus
> every knee should bend

in heaven and on earth and under the earth,
and every tongue should confess
that Jesus Christ is Lord,
to the glory of God the Father.

Guide: Reflect for a few moments on the implications of this song: Jesus had the "form" and power of God. He could have used this divine power to pressure people to accomplish his mission of fashioning the world as God's kingdom. Instead Jesus *emptied* himself of any proud desire to use power in a forceful way. Instead he *took the form of a slave* trying to win over others by loving personal service. *He humbled himself and became obedient to the point of death — even to death on the* cross. This meant that Jesus renounced control over others and risked being powerless to prevent injury to himself from others, even to the point of death. *Therefore God also highly exalted him.* Having emptied himself of pride and self-serving, all of God's power flowed into Jesus. He became a magnet to draw everyone to God by love as their Savior and Lord.

Reflect for a few moments on Jesus' chosen path of compassion and suffering. Feel the love and risk that prompted him to surrender to God's plan. Unite yourself to him in love and ask for the strength to follow in the same way. Meditate on each of the practical suggestions Paul makes: (Texts from Ph 2:3-4). *Do nothing from selfish ambition or conceit.* This practice requires watchfulness over our motives in daily life. Do we speak and act from our heart or are we trying to impress others and win their approval? *In humility, regard others as better than yourselves.* Everyone is unique and with special gifts. Do we respect diversity and realize others have talents or characteristics that we lack? *Let each of you look not to your own interests, but to the interests of others.* Is this the gauge of life's meaning that is most important to us? At the end of each day, let us look back positively upon the times we have thought more about others' interests rather than our own. Let us be grateful for these times and thank God for them. It is God's love in action.

Part II

Mediators of Personal Transformation

6   The Mother Who Was Also Pierced

The gospels present the Mother of Jesus as the companion and guide for understanding the crucifixion of her son. The Gospel of John presents the scene at the foot of the cross with Mary as the central figure:

> Standing near the cross of Jesus was his mother, and his mother's sister, Mary the wife of Clopas, and Mary Magdalen. When Jesus saw his mother and the disciple whom he loved standing beside her, he said to his mother, "Woman, here is your son" (19:25).

In John's gospel, *the disciple whom Jesus loved* also represents the ideal beloved disciple, man or woman. For example, when Lazarus is seriously ill, his sisters send a message to Jesus, "Lord, he whom you love is ill." At the same time, the gospel also notes that Jesus "loved Martha and her sister and Lazarus" (11:5). Accordingly, in order to deeply experience the meaning of the crucifixion, the gospel audience / readers are invited to be at Mary's side at the cross, identifying with her. Together, all observe the painful process of the nailing of Jesus to the cross. After his death, they watch the soldier plunge a spear into Jesus' side and notice how his mother shudders as if it were done to her. With Mary, all gaze at the cross and contemplate the crucifixion. As a reminder to this essential participation, the crucifixion account closes with the words. "They will look on the one whom they have pierced" (19:37). The title of this chapter is drawn from those words.

The gospel of Luke also focuses on the role model of Jesus' mother in regard to the crucifixion. This becomes clear when we remember that the first two chapters are really a mini-gospel describing not only Jesus' birth and childhood but his whole life. Jesus' parents presented him in the temple forty days after his birth. At that time, Simeon blessed them and said to his mother Mary,

> This child is destined for the falling and rising of many in Israel and to be a sign that will be opposed so the inner thoughts of many will be revealed — *and a sword will pierce your own soul, too.*

These words parallel the scene in John's gospel which focussed on the act of crucifixion and those who contemplated it, especially Jesus' mother.

A second reference to Mary's sorrow is found in the story of the losing of the twelve year old Jesus for three days and finding him in the temple. Luke describes the whole incident as a foreshadowing of the death of Jesus and his resurrection after three days. When Jesus' parents found him, his mother said to him, "Child, why have you treated us like this? Look, your father and I have been searching for you in great anxiety" (2:49). The question, "Why have you treated us like this?" conveys a feeling of sorrow. The ancient Latin version reflects this sorrow in translating the next sentence as, "Your father and I have been searching for you with *sorrow (dolentes)."* Luke tells us, "His mother kept all these words in her heart" (literal translation). This hints that Jesus' mother carried a premonition of her son's death in her heart. This is the heaviest burden a mother can carry. The Latin description *dolentes* helped give rise to the description of Mary as *mater dolorosa* (sorrowful mother). This title has been a very meaningful one in the church for almost two thousand years.

Christian tradition continued this gospel portrait of Mary by contemplating her sorrow as the best path to an understanding of the crucifixion. The greatest artists through the centuries have portrayed the sorrowful mother in the cathedrals and churches of the world. The *mater dolorosa* became a special focus of devotion and the subject of songs and poetry. These fulfilled the need of the faithful to arrive at a deeper level of understanding, feeling and awareness regarding the meaning of Jesus' suffering and death.

For almost a thousand years the most popular of these songs / poems has been the *Stabat Mater*. These words literally mean "There stood by (the cross) his mother." These words are taken from the Latin version of John 19:25, "*Stabant*... iuxta crucem Iesu *mater* eius," (There were standing near the cross of Jesus his mother and...). The *Stabat Mater* has been described as the most powerful poem for pathos ever written. It was first sung in the beautiful, simple and moving Gregorian Chant. Then the greatest musicians of the last millennium vied with one another in putting the piece to music. Among them have been Haydn, Rossini, Scarlatti, Palestrina and Pergolesi.

I recently listened to the San Francisco Chamber Music Orchestra play and sing the *Stabat Mater* composed by Pergolesi who wrote it as a young man in 1736 when he was close to his death at the age of 26. As I listened I concluded that the composer must have been more afflicted by his mother's sorrow than by his own. This gave a greater poignancy to his ability to bring the feelings of Jesus' sorrowful mother into his music.

Transforming and Concluding Meditation

I could not choose a better text than the *Stabat Mater* itself. I have arranged it in two columns so the original Latin can be seen side by side with an English translation. Go through it slowly, repeating each verse to yourself with your eyes closed — many times if needed before moving on — until you deeply experience the message and feeling of the song.

STABAT MATER

(Original Latin)	*(English Translation)*
Stabat mater dolorosa juxta crucem lacrymosa dum pendebat filius.	The grieving mother stood weeping beside the cross where her son was hanging.
Cuius animam gementem contristatam et dolentem pertransivit gladius.	Her soul, sighing, anguished and grieving, was pierced by a sword.
O quam tristis et afflicta fuit illa benedicta mater unigeniti!	O how sad and afflicted was that blessed mother of the Only-begotten,
Quae moerebat et dolebat et tremebat dum videbat nati poenas inclyti.	Who mourned and grieved and trembled when she saw the sufferings of her glorious son.
Fac ut ardeat cor meum in amando Christum Deum ut sibi complaceam.	Make my heart burn with love for Christ our Lord, that I may please him.
Sancta mater, istud agas crucifixi fige plagas cordi meo valide.	Holy mother, grant the wounds of the crucified be scored deep in my heart.
Tui nati vulnerati tam dignati pro me pati poenas mecum divide.	Share with me the pains of your wounded son who deigned to suffer so for me.
Fac me vere tecum flere, crucifixo condolere. donec ego vixero.	Make me, Holy One, weep with you, and grieve for the Crucified as long as I live.
Iuxta crucem tecum stare te libenter sociare in planctu desidero.	To stand with you beside the cross and share your grief is my desire.
Virgo virginum praeclara, mihi iam non sis amara, fac me tecum plangere.	Virgin most exalted among virgins be not now ill-disposed towards me, grant that I may grieve with you.
Quando corpus morietur, fac ut animae donetur paradisi gloria.	When my body dies, let my soul be granted the glory of paradise.
Amen.	Amen.

7   The Liturgy and Rituals

The Paschal Liturgy

The Paschal / Easter liturgy is the center of the church's life. Liturgy on Sundays and other days is a renewal and re-experience of it in time. In our presentation of the Last Supper in the gospels and letters of St. Paul, we have shown how the continued celebration of the Lord's Supper is the central mystery of the church. To deepen our appreciation of this mystery, we need to see how the Paschal liturgy presents to us the living image of the risen and crucified Christ. Within this image, there is a special focus on Jesus' five wounds.

On Easter eve, the church is dark and the altar is bare to heighten the contrast between darkness — Christ's absence, and light — his presence. The celebrant enkindles a new fire, struck from the rock of flint. Then he imparts God's blessing on this fire. After this the altar servers bring out a tall beeswax candle and stand it before the people. This represents the human body in which "the Word became flesh and dwelt among us." The celebrant takes a sharp knife so he can carve out a new identity for the candle. This parallels Calvary where the nails and the lance pierced the hands, feet and side of Jesus, our crucified Lord.

First the priest cuts a cross on the side of the candle while saying "Christ yesterday and today" (for the vertical bar) and "the beginning and the end" (for the horizontal bar). Then he inscribes the Greek letters *Alpha* and *Omega* (first and last letters of the Greek alphabet) above and below the cross. Finally he carves four figures for the current year, for example 2000. Then comes a climactic moment. The servers bring up a tray with five large red grains of incense. These are solemnly blessed, incensed and sprinkled with holy water. Then the celebrant, with a piercing action *infixes* each of the five grains on the carved cross to represent the five wounds of Jesus. These are the source of his blood flowing in sacrifice for the loving forgiveness of sin. They signify forever Jesus' new ID as the Risen and Crucified Lord, the Lamb of God who takes away the sins of the world. *The diagram below shows how this all appears on the side of the Paschal candle.*

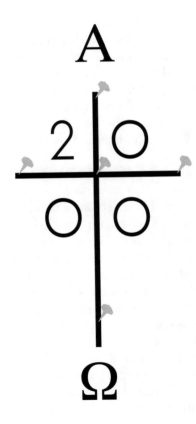

Next the celebrant lights the candle from the new fire, praying at the same time, "May the light of Christ risen in glory scatter the darkness of heart and mind." Now the candle takes on its full meaning as signifying Christ, the source of light and energy for the world. This Light desires to be shared and spread by each one present. So the celebrant and acolytes begin a solemn procession carrying the lighted candle through the church. As they enter, the priest raises the candle and sings, "Light of Christ" (*Lumen Christi* in the Latin ritual). The entire congregation responds, "Thanks be to God" (*Deo Gratias*).

Then the priest lights his own candle from that of the Paschal Candle. Moving further into the church he lifts the candle a second time with the same song and response. This time all the clergy light their candles from the same source. Moving further he lifts the candle a third time and sings as before. Now everyone in the church lights their own candle passing it on from the Paschal Candle source. Finally all the lights in the church are turned on. Each person has become a living paschal candle and light bearer of the crucified Lord with the same ID as Jesus himself. They now carry his supreme message to the world: to change evil into good through forgiveness, compassion and mercy even in the face of hatred and violence. This is the *sign of the cross*. After this, the whole community, holding their lighted candles, stands during the intonation of a beautiful song of praise and gratitude to Christ represented by the blazing Paschal Candle in their midst. He is the Light of the world, destroying the power of darkness and bringing the warmth and light of God's forgiving love to all.

Easter is the special time when new converts are baptized and faithful believers renew their baptismal promises after the Lenten time of preparation. The power of water to bring about this transformation comes from the Risen Christ. So the celebrant plunges the Paschal Candle three times into the basin of water singing each time, "May the power of the Holy Spirit descend into the waters of this font." After the baptisms, the new converts along with the faithful pronounce together their baptismal vows, all holding their lighted candles. The priest reminds them of their new identity and configuration with the crucified and risen Christ by reading this baptismal instruction adapted from St. Paul,

> By baptism we have been buried with Christ. As Christ has risen from the dead, so we too must now walk in the newness of life. For we know that our old self has been crucified with Christ so we may no longer be slaves to sin. Let us, then, remember that we have died to sin, but are to live for God, in Christ Jesus our Lord.

The Paschal Candle During the Year

Outside the Easter season, the Paschal Candle still has a special function. It stands near the altar or baptismal font with its red incense jewels proclaiming the resplendent wounds of the Risen Jesus. It remains beside the altar and is lit during baptisms, funerals and wedding Masses. Along with the large crucifix usually over the altar, it remains the principal image of the crucified Jesus.

Toward More Fervent Participation in the Eucharist

We have already seen that St. Paul wrote to the Corinthians that their celebrations were often not for the better but for worse. He warned them that the table of the Lord cannot be separated from the needs of the poor. Otherwise it could not "proclaim the Lord's death until he comes" (1 Cor 11:26). There are other obstacles too that prevent people from more fruitful participation in the table of the Lord. However, this book would not be the place to go into this in detail. There is one basic preparation that is essential to the meaning of the Table of the Lord. In the Eucharist, there is the privileged opportunity for a deeper and closer union, relationship and identification with the risen Jesus. Something of this magnitude cannot be entered into lightly and with haste. For this reason the gospels focus on Jesus' directions and concern for the preparation of his final Passover meal with his disciples.

Jesus himself *eagerly* looked forward to this occasion. He told his disciples, "I have eagerly desired to eat this Passover with you before I suffer" (Luke 22:15). This tells us that he wants believers to look forward likewise with an *eager desire* to their participation at the Holy Sacrifice of the Mass. This is not merely a one-to-one matter; it concerns other people as well. Jesus also said on this occasion (in Luke's version), "Who is greater, the one who is at the table or the one who serves? Is it not the one at table? But I am among you as one who serves" (22:27). Thus the eager desire for *loving service* of others is part of being identified with Jesus in the Eucharist.

With Matthew's emphasis on identification with Jesus (chapter 2), we can increase our desires for participation and service by extending our image of the crucified Jesus to all those abandoned or suffering like himself. And we can show them Jesus' love and concern.

One common characteristic of all the examples we have given of holy people is that they gave *prime time* to meditation and contemplation of the crucified Jesus. Often they did so in quiet churches or chapels. This has the advantage of all the atmosphere and energy of a *holy place*. When it was not possible for them to do so, they created their own *holy places*. Today, most people do not have the option of a quiet church where they can pray and enjoy spiritual communion with God. Most churches are closed during the day except for the time of services. This is necessary to shield them from vandalism and protect people who might be alone and vulnerable inside. Thus it is all the more important for people to create their own sacred places.

The following are some suggestions along this line. There are many other possibilities also:

1. Find a secret place outdoors that only you know about for this purpose. Francis of Assisi did not receive the stigmata of Jesus

in a quiet chapel but in a cave on Mount Alverno. He spent much of his life outdoors. For him this was God's own great cathedral constantly giving him messages about God's goodness and beauty. In San Francisco in the Arboretum of Golden Gate Park, there is a beautiful grove with a statue of St. Francis. The birds are often found there resting calmly on his shoulders and arms. Living in communion with nature is to live in communion with God.

2. Make your own *holy place* at home. We might object, "But there is no room!" Yet it is interesting that even in tiny one room homes in India millions of families make a little holy place separated by a curtain where individuals may withdraw for private silence and prayer. Place there an image of the cross and any other reminders you wish. A candle perhaps to light — this serves to "turn on" a sacred atmosphere. Spend some prime time there each day for nourishing reading, prayers or meditation. Or write a few words in a private spiritual journal to keep track of your progress.

3. Best of all, in addition to those above, have a *portable* holy place. This can be created by using the *Jesus prayer* described in chapter 3. In today's world an automobile can be a good holy place. There are so many stops from traffic lights, jams and delays that we sometimes have more time available for prayer and meditation driving to work than a monk does in the mountains of Tibet. Even while driving, we can listen to the bible or other fine inspirational books on tape — even free of charge from libraries.

Part III

Examples of Saints
Who Have Borne the Five Wounds
of Jesus, the Stigmata

8 Francis of Assisi, Fool for Christ and First Stigmatic

What follows is an introduction to the life of a man whose simple life-style and devotion to God and the poor set an extraordinary example for generations to come. Francis of Assisi in his striking resemblance to Christ brought the church back to its grass-roots of love and service.

Childhood and Youth

Francis was born to Pietro and Giovanna (called Pica) di Bernardone in Assisi, a small town in the region of Umbria, Italy in late 1181 or early 1182. His father was a very wealthy merchant and dealer in fine cloths. As a teenager, Francis always had a full purse which he disbursed lavishly for good times. Friends looked up to him as the life of any party. Legend relates that he always radiated a spirit of joy and enthusiasm; he was fond of music, song and dance. The *farandole* was the traditional circle dance of the region. Often he led groups singing and dancing it through the city streets until the wee hours of the morning. Even more than his companions, he was considered a great dreamer and enthusiast for the chivalric romantic ideal of those days. Later in life, Francis said of his youth that he "lived in sin" at this time. No doubt his artistic and emotional temperament led him to a few excesses, but there is no evidence of anything more. He loved the outdoors and traveled from place to place taking in all the beauty and enjoyment of a life led to the full.

War with Perugia and Imprisonment

A two year war between Perugia and Assisi began when Francis was eighteen. He joined the little army and fought bravely until the Perugians, having killed many men from Assisi and captured Francis along with several of his companions, decisively defeated them. Francis was thrown into prison where he suffered greatly from the cold and other deprivations. Finally, after a year he was ransomed by his father and returned home limping and supported by a cane. With his mother's loving care he gradually recovered his health. This recuperation period was a time of serious reflection and adjustment. However, once back with his friends he resumed his former carefree lifestyle. He was the *crazy* young man that everyone smiled at and enjoyed.

A Knight in Shining Armor Returns in Failure

At about this time, Pope Innocent III proclaimed a fourth crusade to recover Jerusalem and the Holy Land. To be a knight in this holy crusade was Francis' great desire, a way to fulfill his dream of glory. It was an expensive enterprise requiring a horse, fitted armor and an accompanying squire. To finance this, his father Bernadone sold a farm and Francis set off with a nobleman to join the company of crusaders. For some unknown reason, he turned back and came home. One theory is that he became exhausted and sick with a type of malaria. One of his biographers relates that in a delirious dream he heard a voice telling him to return home and there he would be told what to do. Upon recovery, he sold his expensive armor, bought simple clothes and headed for home.

He was deeply shaken by this disgraceful return and knew his life had to change. He arranged a great feast for his friends to celebrate his homecoming and appeared on the surface to be his old self. Then suddenly, in the midst of the festivities he walked off by himself. His companions found him wandering the streets and thought he was *pazzo,* crazy. They all began to laugh at him and pass the word along. Francis was twenty-five at this time and seeking a new direction in life. He began to go off by himself to pray and give generously to beggars from the abundance in his father's store.

The Talking Crucifix at San Damiano and Rejection by His Father

One day Francis took a long walk and entered an old dilapidated church called San Damiano. Over the altar hung a large crucifix painted with Christ's realistic, vivid wounds. In his own desolate state, Francis identified with the abandoned, suffering figure on the cross. Suddenly he realized the meaning of Jesus' death — his willingness to be nailed to the cross out of compassion and love for others. Francis fell on his knees and tears came to his eyes. Suddenly Christ's image seemed alive and he heard Jesus' voice telling him, "Francis, rebuild my church." From this moment, Christ crucified became the driving force in his life. At first he understood Christ's words as applying to San Damiano, but later learned they referred to the entire Church which badly needed repair and reform due to the loss of spiritual direction he constantly witnessed.

After a pilgrimage to Rome and a period of prayer, Francis knew he must respond to God's call. When his father was away, he sold a large quantity of his father's best scarlet cloth to cover repair expenses at San Damiano. He offered the money there to

an old priest in charge but he would not accept it, so Francis simply left the money in the church. Upon returning home his father
was furious so Francis went into hiding. Finally the young man
returned home and faced his father who was determined to punish him. He wanted restitution for this money plus the cost of ran-
soming him from Perugia and providing him his armor and acces-
sories as a crusader to the Holy Land. At first his father locked
Francis in the house cellar. Then he presented him publicly before the town magistrates, who deferred to the bishop for jurisdic-
tion.

A crowd gathered in the church square for the spectacle. The
bishop gave a short address in which he said, "You have seriously
offended your father. If you wish to serve God, give him back the
money you possess. Perhaps it was ill-gotten and God does not want
you to use it for sacred things. Have courage, act like a man. As
for San Damiano, God will provide." Francis then restored the
purse of money he had brought to San Damiano. Then, before the
shocked onlookers, the young man took off all his clothes one by
one until he stood naked before his father. He then shouted to the
crowd, "Listen everyone, from now on I can say with complete
freedom, 'Our Father who art in heaven.' Pietro Bernadone is no
longer my father. I give him back not only his money but my
clothes as well."

Even the bishop was moved to tears and wrapped Francis in
his episcopal cloak. Some of the crowd pulled out an old shirt and
torn coat from the rubbish heap and gave it to him. He accepted
it with gratitude and later inscribed it with a white cross. Then he
left the city for a few days. As he went away, people heard him
laughing and singing. Now he had become a fool for Christ, as St.
Paul had described himself (1 Cor 4:10).

His Lady Poverty

The custom in those days was for the knights to dedicate
themselves to a special Lady.

Francis had fallen in love with God so he too would have his special "Lady Poverty," as he called her. At that time, due to the ravages of war, homeless beggars roved the countryside going from house to house to ask for alms. Francis resolved to have nothing more than did those who were the poorest of the poor. He would possess nothing of his own and would beg for food and help, but never receive money from others. It is said that he cheerfully accepted what was given him even when some food was unappetizing and even spoiled. Later, poverty would be the matter he insisted on most for those who joined him. He did not want his community to become a settled, secure religious institution like some of the religious orders of the day. Francis' ideal was not simply to possess little or nothing but to welcome the freedom it gave one to be like Jesus, the Son of Man who, unlike the birds of the air who had nests and the wolves of the field who had dens, had nowhere to lay his head. His wealth was the cross itself and his sole desire was to possess everything in God.

Later the rule of St. Francis would enjoin utter simplicity in clothing, possessions and way of life:

> I strictly forbid all friars to accept money on any account, either themselves or through a third person.... Friars are not to acquire any possessions, whether houses, land or anything whatsoever.... They are to ask alms in confidence, nor need they be ashamed to do so, for our Lord made himself poor in this world for our sake. Herein lies the dignity of most noble poverty, which has made you, dearest brothers, poor in worldly goods but rich in virtue. Let poverty be your inheritance, and lead you into the land of the living. Dearest brothers, be completely loyal to poverty, and in the Name of our Lord Jesus Christ have no wish to possess anything under heaven but Him.

Fellow Workers and Community Spirit

Without money to repair San Damiano, Francis went from house to house asking for stones and materials as well as food for himself and other hungry and homeless people. Soon a number of his former companions joined him. Once more they became that joyful singing troupe of energetic youth infected by the enthusiasm of Francis. They also went from house to house, brought stones and materials to San Damiano and, later on, to other churches, where they set to work rebuilding and repairing them. Several became permanent followers of Francis, embracing Lady Poverty along with him. Joyful service was a special characteristic of Francis. Often during a journey he would pick up two sticks, fashion them in the shape of a violin and begin to sing. Even in his last illness he composed a joyful "Canticle to Brother Sun" calling on all creation to joyfully praise God. When he finished it, he assembled his brothers to sing it with him.

Although Francis frequently needed time to be alone for prayer and contemplation, he was most often at the side of other companions. Calling themselves friars they went *two by two* on their travels spreading the good news of God's love. Francis looked upon his companions not merely as fellow crusaders but as real family members. Later his First Rule would read:

> Each friar is to make his wants known to his brother, so that he can obtain his needs. Let each cherish his brother as a mother loves her child, for God will grant him grace to do so…. When any brother falls sick, the others are not to leave him, wherever he may be, unless one or more of them is appointed to look after him as they would wish to be cared for themselves.

Francis himself put this priority of looking to others' needs in practice. On one occasion when the religious family gathered for a day of prayer and meditation, one of the friars was suffering so greatly from hunger that he cried out, "I am hungry." Francis immediately stopped everything and told his companions to prepare a meal for this brother and for everyone.

The Priority of Service to the Desperately Poor, Abandoned and Lepers

Francis was brought up in a wealthy family with all the comforts of life. Yet he realized that those who were avoided, had nothing, and were abandoned were really extensions of the suffering Christ. This was especially true of lepers in his time. They huddled together in abandoned places where the stench of their rotting flesh would not bother others who would force them away if they came near. As a child, Francis had often seen them at a distance and shrank away from their fetid wounds. After his experience at San Damiano, the story is told that he was riding out in the countryside when he heard the familiar clapper sound that lepers used to warn people of their approach. He shuddered and was tempted to turn aside. However a force deep within him made him dismount, approach the leper and kiss his wounds. Then he felt a great joy and the leper reciprocated his greeting. On returning to his horse, he turned around and saw the leper had disappeared. Francis began to sing with joy for realized he had embraced the crucified Christ. On leaving his father's house, he became an attendant at a hospice for lepers. Later on, Francis and his companions made their ministry to lepers one of their priorities.

Clare of Assisi and Franciscan Women

Women were by no means strangers to Francis in his youth. There were women who accompanied his joyful group as they went around town singing and dancing the *farandole*. We may well imagine that he was strongly attracted to them given his very emotional and sensitive nature. They too must have enjoyed his company. However, after his conversion Francis knew his impetuous nature was prone to excesses and that he had to be careful to curb himself. Later in his rule he did not permit his friars to speak with women unless it was a matter of giving them spiritual counsel.

We do not know how well Clare knew Francis before his conversion. In that small town, she must have seen him from time to time and perhaps she was at the town gathering where Francis publicly turned away from his father in order to give himself to God. She was about twelve years old at that time. However, her parents were already discussing marriage prospects for their beautiful daughter. She had led a very sheltered life, spending hours in prayer each day, and putting aside food for the poor from the family table.

Clare suddenly found herself faced with the prospect of marriage when she had determined to give herself completely to God in some form of religious life. She decided to go secretly to Francis and ask for spiritual guidance. He immediately recognized in her a kindred spirit. He listened carefully to her but then put her to a test: If she were really sincere she should go, change her rich clothes, put on an old sack and go begging around town. Despite the difficulty and humiliation, she followed Francis' direction and recognized Lady Poverty as her sister.

Clare knew her parents would not give her permission to do as she desired. So together with her sister Pacifica, she secretly ran away from home at night to the chapel of St. Mary of the Angels where Francis and his friars awaited them. The first step for a friar was tonsure and Francis himself carefully cut her long beautiful hair and that of her sister. Then the women exchanged their rich clothes for the rough and simple Franciscan garb. After this, they recited their first vows of total service to God. Then they took refuge temporarily at a Benedictine convent on the road to Perugia.

In an angry rage, her father and an uncle came with an armed band to seize the two women and bring them home by force. They firmly resisted even after being beaten. Finally the family relented. The bishop gave the sisters the church of San Damiano — the church that Francis rebuilt after Christ spoke to him from the crucifix over its altar — as their new home. The close bond between Francis and Clare continued through the years even though they had few opportunities to see one another. Her devoted prayers and loving support gave him courage throughout his life. During his last illness he asked to be brought near the Sisters' convent so that Clare and a companion could come to minister to his needs each day. Their friendship has been immortalized. Whenever missionaries from Europe went to America, they usually named some town after St. Francis and nearby, another with the name of St. Clare. As I write this from Pacifica, California, I remember that I am located between two cities, San Francisco and Santa Clara.

The Beggar Goes to Rome For Approval

As the number of Friars increased, Francis drew up a Rule to guide their lives in the spirit of the cross and Lady Poverty. Needing official approval for the Rule, Francis decided to go to Rome and present it to the Pope. Innocent III, who was Pope at the time, was very proud of his lofty position as the visible representative of Christ on earth and a temporal ruler even over kings. When he first caught sight of the ragged unknown beggar and his companions, he ordered them to be thrown out. That night the Pope had an unusual dream about a palm tree growing to a fantastic height. The next morning he sent for Francis and his companions and gave them a special audience where Francis explained his Rule to him and a group of Cardinals.

Many of the Cardinals raised serious questions: "How could these Friars live without money?" "Was it not impractical?" "Would not a group of wandering beggars create havoc and disorder in the church?" But one Cardinal spoke in their favor, "To say that this rule is impractical would be to reject the Gospel and blaspheme against Christ." The Pope could hardly disagree with this statement but was also concerned about practicality. He told Francis to pray to Christ to reveal his will to them; afterwards, he might be able to approve their Rule. The Friars went away to pray and returned only to meet with the same objections. The Pope then told them to pray again for inspiration concerning a more sensible Rule.

The determined Francis prayed and came back to see the Pope. Meanwhile Innocent III had another upsetting dream. He saw the Lateran Basilica ready to topple over. However a friar beggar was supporting the church and keeping it from collapsing. The Pope recognized this beggar as Francis. This time, the Pope encouraged Francis, advising him to come back after he had a larger number of friars. He also authorized them to preach — this was quite unusual and very important for Francis and his brothers. Very few of them were priests and some were not highly educated. Francis himself never became a priest, but was eventually ordained a deacon.

Preachers and Missionaries

News of the Pope's approval gave renewed impetus to the preaching mission of the friars. Francis sent them two by two all over Italy, and as their numbers grew, to other countries as well. Their approach was very simple: to preach the good news of the cross with its message of generous forgiveness available to all. Like the cross at San Damiano, church crucifixes took on new meaning as the friars spoke from their hearts about Jesus' five wounds and the suffering he underwent out of love for each one present. The friars preached even more by their actions than by their words. Between sermons they went from house to house begging food for themselves and the poor. They accepted no money. In every town they ministered to those sick who were most avoided and abandoned like Christ on the cross. In particular they cared for lepers, washing and bandaging their sores.

While they took firm stands against evil and corruption, they were careful to respect rich and poor, good and bad, alike. Francis instructed the Friars to be "gentle revolutionaries" and "never to raise their voices in speaking with anyone." As a "fool for Christ," he loved to laugh and joke. When people called him a saint, he would reply that, without God's help, he was quite capable of the greatest of sins.

Mission Impossible to the Holy Land: the Gentle Crusader

The great dream of many Christians of that day was the restoration of Jerusalem and the holy places that had been captured by the Saracens. Francis knew how much evil had resulted from some crusades: even Christian cities had been looted and sacked in their name. In fact, many Christians felt they had more to fear from the Crusades than from the Saracens. Francis proposed what many considered an impossible solution: he and twelve of his friars would go to the east and convert the Sultan and his followers to Christianity so there would be no need for violent military intervention. When Francis arrived at the Crusader camp in Syria, he was thoroughly shocked. The camp had a large population of tramps, thieves, criminals and prostitutes. Francis was convinced that repentance had to start here rather than with the Saracens. So with his companions, he began preaching daily in the camp. Many sudden conversions resulted.

The Crusaders, however, soon underwent a terrible defeat costing them thousands of lives. Francis was now convinced that his first mission was to restore peace. Together with another brother he marched to the Saracen's camp where sentries threatened to decapitate them. At this point Francis and his companion cried out, "Sultan, Sultan," and were taken to his palace. The Sultan was a refined ruler who soon found himself engaged in interesting conversations with Francis. The two men impressed each other but no conversions resulted. Perhaps the Sultan was inwardly moved by Francis, for ten years later he relinquished Jerusalem to the Christians without a single battle.

The Franciscan Rule

When Francis returned to Italy from Jerusalem to Assisi around 1220, he was about 40 years old, but his health was seriously deteriorating. His incurably diseased eyes gave him acute, continuous pain. He felt that his years to live were very limited and was concerned about the future of his friars, now some 6000 in number all over the world. He announced his resignation as head of the congregation and appointed Peter of Catania as his successor. However, he reserved to himself the right to complete his work on the Rule. Some of his associates found the finished rule too long and impractical, so Francis had to make some compromises. However, his great vision still permeated the document and he did not realize how the Franciscan spirit would sweep over the world like a tidal wave in the coming centuries. He took the long journey to Rome to present the revised Rule to Pope Honorius who gave it his approval after some further revisions.

The Stigmata of Jesus' Five Wounds

With the approval of his Rule, the handing over of his leadership to his successor, and the serious state of his health, Francis now felt that he had become more like the crucified Jesus he had seen first at San Damiano. His greatest desire was to become configured and intimately united to his crucified Lord. He needed time to abandon himself to this mystery. For this purpose, Francis and two companions went to Mt. Alverno where he had a favorite hermitage in a mountain cave. There Francis shared with Christ all the abandonment and suffering that he had endured on the cross.

On September 14, 1224 (?), the feast of the Exaltation of the Holy Cross, he and his companion Brother Leo saw two fiery angels come down from heaven bearing an image of the crucified

Christ. They fixed into Francis' hands, feet and side the bleeding imprint of the nails of the crucifixion. He could now say with St. Paul, "I have been crucified with Christ" (Gal 2:19). His inner life of conformity with the crucified Lord was now externalized in the imprints of Christ's own wounds. The wounds continued to bleed until his death. From the moment that he received the stigmata, he had to carefully hide it from the eyes of curious people.

The Canticle of the Sun

Francis' health continued to deteriorate. At his request the Friars brought him near San Damiano, the convent of Clare. For fifty days he was in complete darkness. The slightest light gave his diseased eyes excruciating pain. Clare and the Sisters came to care for him each day. Yet he was not sad or dejected. An inner voice told him, "Rejoice as if you already shared the kingdom." He composed the joyful poem / song, the *Canticle to the Sun* and asked Clare and the brothers to sing it to him each day.

The *Canticle to the Sun* is a great hymn of praise to God for all of nature including animals, birds, plants and human beings. It is really a song that summarizes his whole life. Most of his life was spent outdoors as he and his companions wandered from place to place without a fixed abode. This was not something he merely endured but actually welcomed. Nature was his great cathedral and he loved even the smallest of God's creatures in a very practical way. Animals seemed to lose their natural fear and approach him with confidence. In Golden Gate park, San Francisco, the city honors its namesake with a statue of him on a fountain where birds sit on his shoulder and animals come to drink. His stigmata symbolized not only his configuration to Christ but the openness of his sensitive nature to all of God's creation. For this reason, environmentalists claim him as their special patron saint.

Toward the end of his life, a doctor told him that he had only a short time to live. He summoned all his strength to lift up his arms in joy, saying, "Welcome Sister Death!" He then added the final words to his *Canticle to the Sun*:

> Be praised, my Lord, for our sister, bodily death
> From whom no man living can escape.
> Woe to those who die in sin.
> Blessed are those who are found in your holy will.
> The second death cannot harm them.

Just before dying he blessed his successor and close friend Brother Elias who had given him so much grief over his Rule. He also dictated a special letter to his beloved Clare who was too sick to come to him. On the morning of Sunday, October 4, 1226, he died at his favorite place, La Portiuncula, a small building just outside Assisi which over the years, he had rented along with its chapel dedicated to Our Lady of the Angels for a few fish each year from the abbot of the Benedictines.

9   Catherine of Siena

The fifth wound of Jesus in John's Gospel, the piercing of his heart, has been a favorite source of meditation and spiritual inspiration and energy over many centuries. However, relatively few have moved from deep contemplation to intense involvement in political and religious history to the extent of Catherine of Siena. Even rarer are records of young women with so great an influence on their contemporaries. This amazing young woman profoundly moved European society during her life time. Only 81 years after her death she was canonized a saint. Then in 1970, she was given the prestigious title of Doctor of the Church, a rare distinction for women.

Early Life and Spiritual Development

The external events of Catherine's early life provide few indications of her influential future. However, a strong inner life of prayer gave her the unusual courage she needed in later years. She was born in Siena in 1347, the next to youngest of twenty-five children. Her father was Giacomo di Benincasa, a moderately wealthy dyer and tradesman. Her mother Lapa was the daughter of a local poet. Even as a child Catherine devoted herself to intense prayer and meditation during which she was favored with visions and revelations. She also began ascetical practices to intensify her devotion. Among these was a resolve to become a vegetarian. In addition, she only drank wine that was well watered and finally gave it up altogether at fifteen. At that time, this was a rare choice, except in monastic orders. She also placed rough boards under her comfortable bed.

At the age of seven she dedicated herself entirely to Christ. Years later when her parents were determined to arrange her marriage she kept her resolve despite intense family pressure. Catherine even cut her hair and put on a veiled cap in order to avoid suitors. Her mother was shocked especially since she had such beautiful hair and said to her, "You wretched girl. You may have cut off your hair, but don't think you have succeeded in your purpose. Your hair is bound to grow again, and we will force you to take a husband even if it breaks your heart; you will have no rest until you do what we want you to."

Soon afterwards, Catherine's parents began to openly persecute her. They tried to humiliate her by making her do all the housework in place of the maid. And she willingly did so in order to avoid suitors! They took away her private room and never allowed her to be alone. Every day they heaped insults upon her. Finally they found a suitable young man for her and were determined to force her to marry him. However the young lady maintained her firm stand against the marriage and took all this in stride as an opportunity for personal service to God.

One day she had a vision of St. Dominic to whom she was specially devoted. He appeared to her holding the habit of the Sisters of Penance of St. Dominic. He said, "Daughter, take courage and fear no obstacle, for you will undoubtedly put on this habit as you wish." Catherine told her parents about this and implored them for permission to enter the religious life. They at first refused to do so. Finally, when she was sixteen they gave in and permitted her to become a Dominican Tertiary. This meant she could live a secular life but wear the Dominican habit and follow a modified religious rule.

At first she lived a very solitary and ascetic existence in a small room in her parent's home. The little room became a special place of prayer but also of terrifying temptations. When these seemed insurmountable she received a vision of Christ nailed to the cross with his wounds bleeding. He said to her, "Catherine, my daughter, you see how much I suffered for you. Do not be sad then that you must suffer for me." She replied, "My Lord, where were you when my heart was troubled by all these temptations?" He replied, "I was in your heart." From that time on she made rapid progress in her spiritual life. One day she heard Christ promise her, "I will espouse you to me in faith."

Mission to the World

Christ's promise was fulfilled when Catherine was nineteen and experienced a mystical espousal with Christ. He said to her, "I have determined to celebrate the wedding feast of your soul and to espouse you to me in faith as I promised." Accompanying Christ were Mary the mother of Jesus, John the evangelist, the apostle Paul, St. Dominic (Founder of the Third Order to which she belonged) and the prophet David who played the wedding music. Then Jesus' mother took her by the hand and presented her to Jesus for her spiritual marriage. Jesus held out a precious diamond ring and placed it on her finger saying, "I marry you to me in faith, your Creator and Savior." This spiritual espousal was a preparation for a great new mission in the world.

As a reminder of this event, Catherine always wore this ring on her finger but no one else could see it. Christ made her understand that all this was to prepare her for extraordinary service to the world. After this, she began leaving her home to attend to the sick, even those with repulsive diseases. She also served the poor with whatever help she could get from her parents and others. During a deadly plague in Siena she did not hesitate to minister to those afflicted even at great risk to herself.

It is said that Catherine was a woman of considerable personal charm and joy. At the same time, she was remarkable for her courage and strength in times of crisis. For example, when a young man, Nicolo di Toldo, was sentenced to be beheaded in public, he sent a friend to ask Catherine to come to his execution to give him courage. She went there and awaited his arrival at the place of execution in the public square. There she caressed his head as it lay on the block. Later she wrote to her confessor, Raymond of Capua about what had happened:

> I have just taken a head into my hands and have been moved so deeply that my heart cannot grasp it.... I waited for him at the place of execution... He arrived like a meek lamb and when he saw me he began to smile. He asked me to make the sign of the cross over him.... I stretched out his neck and bent over him, reminding him of the blood of the Lamb. His lips kept murmuring only "Jesus" and "Catherine," and he was still murmuring when I received his head into my hands.... My soul rested in peace and quiet, so aware of the fragrance of blood that I did not remove the blood that had splashed on me.

Catherine attracted a group of men and women of similar mind who worked alongside her ministering to the sick and poor. Soon the little group began suffering persecution and opposition not only from townspeople but even from members of her own religious community. Fortunately the Dominicans assigned Raymond of Capua as a special guide and confessor to her. He became Catherine's trusted friend and helped her through many difficult times. Raymond later became the superior general of the Dominican Order.

Catherine's special source of strength was daily Mass and Communion along with meditation and identification with the crucified Jesus. One day, when she was again severely troubled by temptations, Jesus appeared to her showing his five wounds. In the vision, he invited her to drink from the water flowing from his side. Doing so, she experienced a renewed strength and courage after the ordeals she had suffered. Later, during a visit to Pisa she fell into ecstasy after Holy Communion and told her confessor,

> You must know, Father that by the mercy of the Lord Jesus I now bear in my body his stigmata. I saw the Lord fixed to the cross coming toward me in a great light… then from the scars of his most sacred wounds I saw five rays of blood coming down towards me, to my hands, my feet and my heart. Realizing what was to happen, I exclaimed, "O Lord God, I beg you — do not let these scars show on the outside of my body!" As I said this, before the rays reached me their color changed from blood red to the color of light, and in the form of pure light they reached the five points of my body, hands, feet and heart.

Her confessor asked if she still felt pain at those points now. She replied, "I feel such pain at those five points, especially in my heart, that if the Lord does not perform another miracle, I do not see how I can possibly go on, and within a few days I will be dead." Her confessor and others there at the time prayed intensely that her life would be spared her. The next time she received Holy Communion, she gave no signs of suffering the usual pains, so her confessor asked whether she still felt the pain. She replied, "The Lord, to my great displeasure, has granted your prayers, and those wounds no longer give my body any pain; instead they have made it stronger and healthier and I can feel quite clearly that the strength comes from the places where the agonies were before."

This experience of the stigmata intensified Catherine's union with him and gave her courage for the public apostolate she was beginning. Her vast correspondence to popes, kings and people of influence began. The object of her letters was to heal the factions causing civil war in her own country, to influence Pope Gregory to return to Rome from Avignon, and to reform the church. She even wished to start a new crusade to regain the Holy Land by uniting the European powers.

Accompanied by a small group of followers who supported her, in 1376 she journeyed to Avignon, France as an ambassador of Florence to persuade the Pope to return to Rome. She made such an impression on the Pope that he returned to Rome the next year despite much opposition from the French king and most of the College of Cardinals. During his return trip the Pope stopped a month at Genoa where Catherine and her companions came to see him. Among her companions were two young men who acted as the secretaries to whom she dictated her growing correspondence. They later dedicated themselves to God in the religious life.

In 1378, the pope sent Catherine as an ambassador to Florence in order to obtain a peace treaty. The opposition to this peace was so great that an attempt was made on her life. Her response was that she regretted losing the opportunity to be a martyr! Even faithful followers advised her to leave the city. Catherine listened to them and accepted their good intentions but said that she would never leave the city until her mission of peace was accomplished and a treaty was entered into.

During a later schism in the church there were two claimants to the papacy. This came about because Gregory XI, the seventh pope of French nationality, died in Rome in 1378. The people of Rome clamored to the assembled Cardinals for an Italian Pope and Urban VI was elected. However, the Cardinals became upset when Urban began reforms and proved too strict for their taste. So the Cardinals gathered again, nullified the previous election and chose instead the Cardinal of Geneva who took the name Clement VI. Clement retreated to Avignon and was supported by France, Spain, Scotland and Sicily, while Italy and the rest of Christendom remained under Urban in Rome.

Catherine supported Urban VI who called her to Rome. She made the journey with a large number of men and women in order to assist the Pontiff. They obtained food and shelter by begging along the way. In Rome, Catherine worked assiduously for the reform of the church, serving the poor and destitute. At the same time, under the Pope's direction, she wrote letters trying to heal the schism. This heavy apostolate drained her strength but she asked God to accept her sufferings for the sins of the world and to bring about the unity and reformation of the church. The schism did not end until 1424 at the council of Constance when Martin V was elected Pope and peace was restored to the church. By that time Catherine was already dead for 44 years, but she had provided the groundwork for the church's healing.

Catherine's public life was a remarkable contrast to her quiet private life. In public, she was anything but shy and retiring. She was bold and direct even omitting the usual polite expressions in order to increase the impact of her words. She once wrote to three Cardinals who were supporting the anti-pope: "What made you do this? You are flowers who shed no perfume, but a stench that makes the whole world reek." When Gregory XI expressed the fear that he would be poisoned if he left Avignon and returned to Rome, she wrote to him, "Don't be a timid child, but manly." At the same time she wrote to him affectionately as a devoted daughter, calling him in Italian, "Babbo" equivalent to "Daddy."

Her written works comprise about four hundred letters, the *Treatise on Divine Providence* and a collection of *Prayers*. Her correspondence was so extensive that at times she had three secretaries working for her. Her profound knowledge and the influence of her writings prompted the Pope to name her a doctor of the church in 1970. Thanks to a contemporary biographer in the person of her confessor and spiritual director Raymond of Capua, we have valuable first hand information about her.

Whenever Catherine was exhausted and worn out by severe pain, she offered her sufferings to Christ for the peace and reconciliation of the church. Near the end of her life, despite her weakness and confinement to her home, she arose early each morning for the long walk to St. Peter's for morning Mass until a few days before her death. Her final political triumph was the reconciliation of Urban VI with the Roman Republic shortly before her death in 1380 at the age of 33.

10   Padre Pio

In May, 1999, at a solemn ceremony in St. Peter's, Pope John Paul II presided over the beatification of a spiritual son of St. Francis, Padre Pio. This is the final step leading to his canonization as a saint of the Church. I feel amazed as well as privileged that I was able to see him and speak with him while he was still alive.

This took place almost fifty years ago, but I remember it as clearly and vividly as if it were yesterday because of the deep impression it made on me. I did not go to see him with great expectations that might have affected my reactions; our meeting was almost accidental. At the time, I was studying in Rome. While in Italy, I often visited relatives on both sides of my family. My father emigrated to America when he was twelve years old and my mother was born of Italian parents while they lived in France. My grandmother's brother, Luigi Di Nunzio lived in Manfredonia on the Adriatic coast and I made plans to visit him in the spring of 1950.

I realized that Padre Pio lived in the mountainous little town of San Giovanni Rotondo not far from Foggia, the railroad terminal where I would stop to change trains for Manfredonia. I decided to pay an overnight visit to San Giovanni and stay for Padre Pio's Mass on the next morning. The news I had previously heard about him was ambivalent. Some considered him a genuine saint; others thought that the tales about him were simply unbelievable — especially that he bore the five wounds of Jesus, the stigmata, on his body. There were also stories of bi-location along with extraordinary miracles and healings. I knew that church authorities were very cautious in commenting about him.

At one time the distrust of church authorities was so great that Padre Pio encountered opposition not only from his Capuchin superiors but even from local clergy and the Vatican itself. Some suggested that he was a victim of superstition, autosuggestion, hysteria or even diabolical possession. Some priests maintained that the faithful should not be attached to just one person but to their local parish leaders. Padre Pio's miracles were often dismissed as mere superstition and exaggerated tales. At one time in his life, church authorities severely clamped down on him. For ten years, they restricted his contacts with the outside world. At times, he was not allowed to celebrate Mass publicly or hear confessions. For long stretches of time he was not even permitted to correspond with persons outside the monastery.

These ten years were the most difficult in his life. The church he so loved denied him the ministry to which he had dedicated his life. With even the opposition of some in his own community, he felt that he was an outcast whose existence was barely tolerated. These interior wounds were much more painful than the exterior stigmata. With more time on his hands he devoted himself to deeper meditation on the cross. He now felt that he shared Jesus' own acute sense of abandonment when he was denied by Judas and Peter and deserted on the cross. He must have been tempted as Jesus to think that God had abandoned him when he cried out from the cross, "My God, my God, why have you forsaken me?" (Mark 15:34). This sharing of Jesus' darkest moments increased Padre Pio's sense of identification with his wounds and crucifixion.

Realizing that doubts existed about Padre Pio's authenticity, I wanted to see and decide for myself. I arrived at San Giovanni Rotondo toward the evening. It was very cold with a light snow on the ground. I asked around for a place to stay and was directed to the home of a woman who took in boarders. I told her that I had come to see Padre Pio and I could see she had a great reverence for him. When I asked about the cost of lodging and breakfast, she quoted a very nominal sum. However, seeing that I was a young student, she waived this and asked that I remember her and her family at the Mass. She said that I needed to arrive at the parish church while it was still dark at about five in the morning. Padre Pio would offer Mass after he finished hearing confessions. She offered to awaken me in time in the morning. Very early next morning she knocked on my door and brought me *cafe latte* (coffee mixed with milk) and bread rolls.

On entering the church, I found it packed with people not only from the town but (as I learned later), from all parts of Italy and even foreign countries. Long lines of people were waiting to enter Padre Pio's darkened confessional to confess their sins or receive counsel from the Padre. (In Italy, monks are addressed as "Padre," (Father) while other priests are addressed by their first name, preceded by "Don." Some confessions were very long and it was an hour and a half before Padre Pio emerged to prepare for Mass. Hearing confessions and acting as a spiritual director was his principal ministry. Over the years, many thousands sought his confessional. He gave unselfishly of his time which usually meant most of the day. People felt he really listened to them and offered a compassionate understanding of their needs and problems. Tales went around that at times he could even read their minds or remind them of things unsaid or hidden.

For Padre Pio the Mass was the central event of each day. This was true as well for the many pilgrims who had taken great pains to reach this out of the way town. The Mass was the renewal of the sacrifice of the cross, the focal point of Padre Pio's life. He usually arose hours beforehand to say his prayers in preparation for its celebration. People believed that his Mass was especially meaningful because he was so closely identified with the crucified savior bearing, as he did, the wounds of Jesus in his hands and feet. In addition, people felt that he carried their wounds in his heart and deeply felt their own suffering. His ten years of rejection and isolation only increased his sense of deep compassion for the inner wounds and suffering of others.

At his Mass, I noticed that he wore a long white alb with extra length sleeves so these wounds could not easily be seen. However, after the consecration, when he lifted up the Host for adoration the sleeves slipped down enough so that I and the congregation could see the stigmata on his hands. His Mass was at least twice as long as an ordinary Mass, even though there was no sermon on weekdays. He pronounced the Latin prayers slowly and with great devotion with his back to the people (as always before Vatican II). At times he stopped and became transported in ecstasy; a usually short prayer might take five minutes or more. Another great moment was Holy Communion when his outstretched hand revealed an imprint of one of Jesus' five wounds. After the Mass the Padre spent a long period of prayer and thanksgiving attending another Mass offered by another friar. Many people remained in church to pray with him.

After Padre Pio left the church, I went outside to the Piazza to warm myself in the sun and chat with some of the people who had gathered there. I happened to speak with an Italian gentleman who was very gracious and asked me where I was from and what were my impressions of my visit. He then asked me if I would like to talk with Padre Pio. I declined since I knew that there must be great demands on his time from the many pilgrims. However he told me not to worry. He then said that he was Padre Pio's brother and would gladly bring me to visit him.

We walked to the adjoining monastery of Santa Maria delle Grazie, where his brother led me up a flight of stairs to the Padre's room and knocked on the door. I was worried that this might be an intrusion, but Padre Pio answered the door and welcomed his brother and myself into his small, barely furnished cell. His brother introduced me and Padre Pio approached to warmly shake my hand. I noticed that he was wearing protective light gloves and I was careful not to squeeze his hand lest I offer him additional pain. Despite my "intrusion," Father Pio was genuinely interested in me. He asked me where I was from and about my family. On hearing I was studying in Rome, he asked questions about my studies. He seemed willing to talk to me even longer, but I excused myself, knowing that others were waiting to see him. Usually, visitors except for family and priests, were not allowed to come to his monastery cell so I felt privileged to be brought there. I left after asking for his prayers and kneeling for his blessing. My impression of this brief visit was that of a warm, sensitive, deeply human being. At the time of my visit he was sixty-three years old and I was twenty-eight.

Later I reflected that here was a true son of St. Francis, the first known person to receive the stigmata some six centuries before. Padre Pio, Francesco Forgione, was born in 1887 at Pietralcina in one of the most backward areas of southern Italy. His parents were so poor that his father (like my own) had to emigrate to America. Padre Pio's father went to Brooklyn, New York (which Italians called "Brocolino") to earn money to support the family. Another surprise was that his mother's maiden name was the same as mine — Di Nunzio. And her first name, like my own was Giuseppa (Joseph/ine)

As a young man, Francesco was distinguished by his religious devotion and entered the Capuchin branch of the Franciscan family as a novice, intending to study for the priesthood. In Rome, I had met several Capuchins in my classes. They came to class in the coldest weather barefooted with sandals. Their monasteries were unheated. I noticed that they liked to go out in the sunshine after class in order to warm up. Padre Pio was once asked why he picked the Capuchins. With his typical sense of humor he responded, "I liked their beards."

The ascetic life of the monastery along with his poor health proved too much for the young Francesco and he had to interrupt his studies several times in order to recuperate. Finally he was ordained, but his illness was diagnosed as tuberculosis. He was unable to take on a regular ministry, but had to stay at home for about six years where he continued his devotion to prayer, contemplation and an ascetic life as well as some limited ministry. After this he did some parish work for a time at Foggia. At the age of 31 in

1918, his superiors transferred him to the monastery of Santa Maria delle Grazie, close to the town of San Giovanni Rotondo. There he remained in that secluded atmosphere until his death in 1968.

The Stigmata

When people mention Padre Pio, they usually refer to his *stigmata* (marks, imprints of Jesus' wounds). In his case these were five open, frequently bleeding, wounds on his body, corresponding to those of Jesus. They did not appear suddenly but developed over a period of years. When alone at home, during the young priest's years of debilitating illness he devoted himself to prayer and meditation on the cross and sufferings of Jesus. Since he was often in pain and misunderstood, he could also more readily identify with the interior pain of Jesus on the cross in his acute feeling of abandonment by his friends and apostles. The young monk felt especially identified with the crucified Jesus and gradually he experienced what is known as the *hidden stigmata*. These are pains at the physical locations corresponding to Jesus' wounds, but without any exterior sign of them.

Soon after his return to the monastery of Santa Maria delle Grazie, one of the friars found him lying on the floor in front of the crucifix in the chapel where the community had their prayers. It was a place where he often came to pray and meditate on the passion and cross of Jesus. The friar who found him helped him return to his cell. There he was extremely embarrassed and the friar utterly amazed to discover that his hands and feet were pierced and bleeding with intense pain. There was also a wound in his side near his heart. These wounds remained continually visible as if freshly inflicted for fifty years. For some mysterious reason they disappeared just before his death in 1968.

The news of his stigmata spread around the world and prompted mixed reactions. To many believers, it was a sign that he was a saint. To others, especially in the scientific world, it was discredited either as a hoax or attributed to hysteria or mental disturbance.

John McCaffery in his book, *Saints are Now* relates that he was deeply impressed by a book written by a Roman physician who was assigned to make a medical study of Padre Pio's stigmata. McCaffery writes as follows:

> He (the physician) had begun as a contemptuous unbeliever in the seriousness of what he had been asked to investigate, but in more than two hundred pages covering a two year period he gave a detailed account of his experiments to find a humanly explicable cause for these stigmata, and ended with a confession of failure and the conclusion that their origin and continuance could be ascribed only to benignly preternatural intervention. He became a devoted disciple of the man whose wounds and whose psychology he had coldly, methodically and often most harshly probed. (p. 102)

It is extraordinary, yet hard to believe that he bore those wounds for over fifty years. They were especially painful when he used his hands or walked on his wounded feet.

Daily Life and Activities

His daily life and activities were quite ordinary as looked upon from the outside, but extraordinary for those who were interiorly moved and changed by him. As said earlier, his daily Mass was the center of his life in his configuration with Christ and the interior source of his strength and courage. Many hours each day were spent in a small confessional where the most important work of his life was done in assuring people of forgiveness and guiding their spiritual journey. This was his best way of reaching out to the world. The hard wooden confessional could be extremely cold in the unheated mountain church. Or it could be blazing hot under the summer sun of southern Italy. The physical endurance it required to remain there was enormous.

His other duties involved being spiritual director of the community for many years. In the afternoon he led a public service of Benediction of the Blessed Sacrament in the church. Above all, his time was taken up with the never-ending line of people from all over the world who stopped him at every turn in the church, sacristy, in the monastery and sometimes in his cell to ask his help or his blessing. This might be for his prayers in difficult situations or healing in sickness. He never turned anyone away without special encouragement. Whatever time he might have left for himself was given to quiet prayer or contemplation in the church or in his room. Rosary beads were a constant companion on his fingers for prayers at odd moments.

Because of his own illness in his youth and his experience with suffering — especially that of the ever present wounds, he was particularly caring toward the sick. Many people reported cures that they attributed to his prayers or blessing. To extend his care for the sick, he devoted much of the last twenty years of his life to constructing and directing a large hospital. When I visited the monastery in 1950, people pointed out the large unfinished structure to me. When Padre Pio first came up with the idea, people thought he was surely dreaming. The location was isolated; communications were lacking; there was no professional labor available nor qualified personnel. Above all there was no money in this poverty stricken area, especially soon after the Second World War.

None of these obstacles phased him. He asked an architect without a degree to design it and a country doctor to supervise the construction. However, to everyone's surprise, as soon as the news of the ridiculous project spread, funds began to pour in from all over the world. Finally a large hospital with hundreds of beds was constructed and outfitted with the best up-to-date modern medical equipment and a staff of excellent doctors and nurses. When it was inaugurated it was also the site of an international cardiac convention. Doctors and professionals arrived from over all the world, among them Paul White, President Eisenhower's consultant. People were deeply moved not only by the hospital but by the humble saintly friar who made it possible. John McCaffery relates that Paul White was so moved by the occasion that he gave a congratulatory speech ending with "And congratulations, Padre, on your wounds!"

Wonder and Controversy

Even after authorities ended their ten year silencing of Padre Pio and after his death in 1968 there has been controversy about this unusual man. Ordinary people were convinced of his holiness and wanted to see him officially canonized. There was proof of all the necessary miracles that were needed. Yet church authorities were hesitant about giving him official approval. They were worried that many might believe the many hundreds of tales of extraordinary miracles that had spread about him, some of them so unusual that they overshadowed even many of Jesus' own miracles in the gospels. Yet they realized, too, that his blessings, prayers and faith had brought healing to countless sick people.

Among the most unusual stories collected in John McCaffrey's book *Tales of Padre Pio* were those of Padre Pio's apparent bi-location. Some of course became quite exaggerated as they spread around. The most unusual of these is the story that during World War II Padre Pio suddenly appeared in the sky to turn back an American bombing mission on its way to bomb San Giovanni Rotondo! Putting aside legends such as this, there are still many testimonies of people who have seen Padre Pio in times of crisis or illness while he was hundreds or thousands of miles away in San Giovanni Rotondo. Must rationality be suspended or hallucination of the recipient be supposed?

I don't think so. What follows is an explanation which may fit the situation and offers no obstacle to his canonization.

Beginning from my own limited experience of him of Padre Pio, I have a vivid memory even after almost fifty years. Those who knew him better than I testify that Padre Pio made an indelible impression on them. They said that he resembled Christ himself. The identifying characteristic of Jesus after his resurrection was his five wounds. When Padre Pio carried these on his body along with his sincere and warm personal service to people in need this created a deep and unforgettable image of him on their minds. At a time of crisis later on, even when long distances away, this image came back to them. For some, it was so strong that it produced a sense of his presence that was so palpable, so unmistakable, as to be almost visual.

My last statement is strong and I wish to verify it. I worked as a volunteer bereavement counselor for a number of years with Hospice of the Valley in San Jose, California. To help those who had suffered severe family losses, we held a weekly group meeting so those recently bereaved could freely share their experience with others in similar situations. Often people mentioned hesitatingly that they had actually seen or heard words from their deceased spouses or family members. They also frequently said that they rarely told anyone else of these experiences lest people think they were crazy or disturbed. However in the atmosphere of people like themselves, they felt free to do so.

With my own academic background, I wanted to verify whether what I had witnessed in these groups were exceptional cases or were they a more general phenomenon. I searched through hospice journals to see if such stories were ever observed or discussed. I was pleased to find studies by nurses that such phenomena were commonly brought up by members of bereavement discussion groups. The image of their deceased at times was so strong and so emotionally powerful that they could truthfully say they actually saw or spoke with their loved ones.

Certainly Padre Pio was a walking image of Christ not only in his external wounds but also in his dedicated service and love for people. In this he also resembled Francis of Assisi, founder of his community centuries earlier, and the first recorded stigmatic. Francis appealed to so many people because he was so much like Christ himself. The same can be said of Padre Pio. Even though he has not yet been officially canonized by the Church, he has been unofficially canonized in the hearts of those thousands of people who knew him. He is the first and only known priest known to have received the stigmata. When he died in 1968, 100,000 people came to his funeral, and even more attended his beatification on May 2, 1999.

When the cause for his canonization is studied, the fact that he had the stigmata will not be a contributing factor. The examiners look at holiness of life and a life of loving service. Actually there have been hundreds of cases of reported stigmatics; relatively few of them are well authenticated and fewer still have been canonized. For this book we have selected the first, St. Francis of Assisi, St. Catherine of Siena, one of the three outstanding women doctors of the church, and finally Blessed Padre Pio. All had a special devotion to the five wounds of Jesus and all of them were conformed to him in an even more profound way, namely, in their love and service of God, the church and their fellow human beings. In the latter, at least, we can all seek to imitate them in the hopes of one day joining them among the blessed of heaven.